GENERAL ANTHROPOLOGY

DANTES/DSST* Test Study Guide

All rights reserved. This Study Guide, Book and Flashcards are protected under the US Copyright Law. No part of this book or study guide or flashcards may be reproduced, distributed or stored in a retrieval system, or transmitted in any form or by any means, electronic, mechanical, photocopying, recording, or otherwise, without the prior written permission of the publisher Breely Crush Publishing LLC.

© 2026 Breely Crush Publishing, LLC

DSST is a registered trademark of Prometric and its affiliated companies, and does not endorse this book.

97107142043

Copyright ©2003 - 2026, Breely Crush Publishing, LLC.

All rights reserved.

This Study Guide, Book and Flashcards are protected under the US Copyright Law. No part of this publication may be reproduced, distributed or stored in a retrieval system, or transmitted in any form or by any means, electronic, mechanical, photocopying, recording, or otherwise, without the prior written permission of the publisher Breely Crush Publishing, LLC.

Published by Breely Crush Publishing, LLC
10808 River Front Parkway
South Jordan, UT 84095
www.breelycrushpublishing.com

ISBN-10: 1-61433-695-4
ISBN-13: 978-1-61433-695-2

Printed and bound in the United States of America.

**DSST is a registered trademark of Prometric and its affiliated companies, and does not endorse this book.*

Table of Contents

Methodologies and Disciplines *1*
   Physical Anthropology *1*
   Cultural Anthropology *3*
   Linguistics *5*
   Archaeology *5*
   Applied Anthropology *6*
History and Theory *8*
   Ethnographies and Perspectives *8*
   Sex and Gender *9*
   Race and Ethnicity *9*
   Cultural Ecology and Evolution *11*
Physical Anthropology *14*
   Genetic Principles *14*
   Human Variation *15*
   Adaption *16*
   Population Genetics *16*
   Evolution of Primates *17*
   Evolutionary Principles *17*
   Variation *18*
   Selection *19*
   Connectivity *19*
   Eco-Evolutional Dynamics *19*
   Primatology *20*
   Western Primatology *20*
   Japanese Primatology *21*
   Primatology in Sociobiology *21*
   Paleontology *22*
   History of Life *24*
Archaeology *26*
   Methodology *26*
   Stratigraphic Methods *26*
   Scientific Methods *27*
   Chronological Methods *27*
   Paleolithic and Mesolithic *27*
   Distribution of Humans *28*
   Tools *29*
   Fire *30*
   Neolithic *30*
   Development of Civilization and Urban Societies *31*

Cultural Systems and Processes *32*
    Components of Culture *32*
    Symbols *33*
    Language *33*
    Values and Beliefs *34*
    Norms *34*
    Symbolic Systems *35*
    Language and Communication *35*
    Human Nonverbal Communication *36*
    Proxemics *36*
    Chronemics *36*
    Kinesics *36*
    Posture *37*
    Gesture *37*
    Eye Contact *37*
    Sign Language *37*
    Verbal Language *38*
    Sapir-Whorf Hypothesis *38*
    Cultural Diffusion and Power *38*
    Cultural Universals *40*
    Sub-Cultures *40*
    Counter-Cultures *40*
    World Systems *41*
    Colonialism *42*
    Arts *42*
    Brief History of Notable Art Discoveries *43*
    Marriage and Family Patterns *44*
    Origin of Family Through World Cultures *45*
    Kinship and Descent Groups *46*
    Family Structures *47*
    Culture and Marriage *48*
    Social and Economic Stratification *48*
Bands, Tribes, Chiefdoms & States *49*
    Bands *50*
    Tribes *50*
    Chiefdoms *52*
    States *53*
    Subsistence and Settlement Patterns *54*
Trade, Reciprocity, Redistribution *55*
    Trade *55*
    Reciprocity *56*

Redistribution *56*
Market Exchange *57*
Modern Political Systems *57*
Globalization and the Environment *58*
Belief Systems *58*
Fundamentalism *59*
Orthodoxy *59*
Modernism/Reform *59*
Mythology *60*
Formal Institutions *60*
Information Organizations *61*
Religious Practices and Practitioners *62*
Rituals *63*
Formalism *64*
Traditionalism *64*
Invariance *64*
Rule Governance *64*
Sacrifice *65*
Performance *65*
Applied Anthropology *65*
Cultural Preservation *67*
Directed Cultural Change *68*
Spontaneous Cultural Change *68*
Environment *69*
Cultural Resource Management *70*
Indigenous Survival and Global Culture *71*
Sample Test Questions *73*
Test Taking Strategies *99*
What Your Score Means *99*
Test Preparation *100*
Legal Note *100*

METHODOLOGIES AND DISCIPLINES

The scientific study of humans, how they behave, and their societies is known as anthropology. It is the study of mankind, both past and present. Anthropology has several methodologies and disciplines that include physical, cultural, and linguistic, along with applied anthropology and archaeology.

 ## Physical Anthropology

Physical or biological anthropology focuses on the biological and behavioral aspects of humans, their hominid ancestors, and non-human related primates from an evolutionary point-of-view. Anthropology, by itself, is the study of humans from a biological perspective.

Physical anthropology, as a subfield, is divided into several branches that have one aspect in common—to understand human behavior and/or biology by applying an orientation/application of the evolutionary theory.

- Bioarchaeology studies past human cultures by examining human remains that were uncovered in an archaeological context. These human remains generally only contain bone fragments, but soft tissue may be preserved as well. Bioarchaeology combines the skills from human osteology, paleopathology, and archaeology, and typically considers the mortuary and cultural context of the discovered remains.
- Evolutionary biology studies the evolutionary processes that started from a single ancestor of common descent. The processes included in evolutionary biology are natural selection, common descent, and speciation.
- Evolutionary psychology studies and works to identify human psychological traits that are evolved. It looks at these traits from a modern perspective, at whether they are the products of natural selection or sexual selection due to human evolution.
- Forensic anthropology is most often used in criminal cases. It applies both the science of physical anthropology and human osteology. Osteology is the study of human bones and is applicable since most of the victims studied are in advanced stages of decomposition.
- Human behavioral ecology (HBE) studies humans' adaptive responses to environmental stress—developmentally, genetically, and physiologically.
- Human biology is an interdisciplinary field that uses practices from biology, biological anthropology, nutrition, and medicine. It looks at the global population

and gains perspectives on the effect that health, evolution, anatomy, physiology, molecular biology, neuroscience, and genetics have on humans worldwide.

- Paleoanthropology studies human fossils for evidence of human evolution. Its main focus is on extinct hominoids and species of primates to determine morphological and behavioral changes in humans, along with the environment in which the evolution occurred.

- Paleopathology studies diseases in antiquity. Not only are bones and soft tissue examined but also the evidence of nutritional issues, and evidence of physical injury/trauma and/or occupational biomechanic stress. Variations in bone stature or morphology over time are also studied.

- Primatology studies non-human primate behavior, genetics, and morphology, along with phylogenetic methods, to determine which traits are shared between humans and primates and which adaptations are specific to humans.

Physical anthropology is an evolving field. Even over the last twenty years, it has changed, including its name. Changed to biological anthropology, scientists in the field often point to Charles Darwin as one of its primary founders with his theory of evolution, but intellectual genealogy and cultural studies can be traced back to Plato (circa 428–347 BCE).

Plato, a Greek philosopher, placed humans on the scala naturae, or the Great Chain of Being. The philosopher created a hierarchy, with the Greek gods placed at the top, and progressed down to angels, humans, animals, plants, and minerals. For over two thousand years, this hierarchy was believed to be true. Aristotle (circa 384–322 BCE), one of Plato's students, observed in his book, History of Animals, that humans were the only species to walk continually upright. He went on to theorize that according to his view, humans have buttocks without tails so they would be able to sit comfortably when they were tired of standing.

He used different climates in other regions to explain the variations in human features and skin color. This characterization of humans that base their character on physical features is known as physiognomy and was first postulated by Hippocratic Corpus. Scientific anthropology was started in the seventeenth and eighteenth centuries, which used physiognomy (racial classification), with leaders in the field being Georgius Hornius, Carl Linnaeus, Francois Bernier, and Johann Friedrich Blumenbach.

Johann Friedrich Blumenbach (of Gottingen) was the first physical anthropologist. A German physician (1752–1840), he gathered a large collection of human skulls which he argued could be divided into five major races. His Decas Craniorum, published in the late 1700s and early 1800s, argued that humans could be separated into Caucasian, Mongolian, Aethiopian, Malayan, and American. While Blumenbach focused on cranial shape, along with Paul Broca (1824-1880) and other French physical anthropologists, Rudolf Virchow (1821–1902) followed the German tradition of studying how disease and environment affected the body.

By the 1830s and 1840s, physical anthropology was being prominently used in slavery debates. British abolitionist James Cowles Prichard's (1786–1848) scientific monogenist works stated all humans derived from a common ancestor, against Samuel George Morton (1799–1851), an American polygenist that believed that there was a different ancestor for each of the five races.

It wasn't until the late 1800s that German-American Franz Boas (1858–1942) introduced the theory that culture and experience influenced human forms. His research went on to show that a human skull is malleable and not a stable trait of a race. Environment and nutrition can affect the shape of the skull. Boas' research did not go unchallenged. Racism still existed in the anthropology community with Earnest Hooton and Aleš Hrdlička, who promoted theories of racial superiority, along with the origination of modern humans in Europe.

A former student of Hooton's, Sherwood Washburn changed the focus of physical anthropology from racial typology to human evolution in 1951. He moved the study away from racial classification to the evolutionary process. Physical anthropology was expanded to include primatology and paleoanthropology. During the twentieth century, Charles Darwin's theory of evolution was reconciled with Gregor Mendel's heredity-focused research. Termed modern syntheses, it was outlined in Julian Huxley's book, Evolution: The Modern Synthesis, published in 1942. Accuracy in understanding past and present humans was also available in greater detail by the mid-twentieth century due to advances in understanding the molecular structure of DNA and in the methods used for chronological dating. This became what was then called "new physical anthropology."

Cultural Anthropology

This branch of anthropology studies cultural differences in humans. Cultural anthropology is a contrast to social anthropology. It is the dominant field of thinking in Europe and the British Commonwealth that theorizes cultural variations are posited, or a predetermined constant.

Cultural anthropology looks to see if these differences are the result of the environment. It is more "hands-on" than social anthropology that theorizes society influences culture, not the environment. Cultural anthropologists often observe the culture. Referred to as "fieldwork," these observers not only immerse themselves into the culture but also conduct surveys and interviews when deemed appropriate and necessary for research.

It is believed that the term "cultural" took on meaning for anthropology from Sir Edward Tylor's 1871 book. On the first page he wrote, "Culture, or civilization, taken in its broad, ethnographic sense, is that complex whole which includes knowledge, belief, art, morals, law, custom, and any other capabilities and habits acquired by man as a member of society." An Australian anthropologist specializing in European prehistory, V. Gordon Childe, advanced the definition of "civilization" to have culture become a type of top tier term and civilization becoming a type of culture. For example, cultures would be considered civilized based on their level of civilization.

Cultural anthropology rose in prominence during the late nineteenth century. Questions were being asked by Karl Marx and Sigmund Freud and others, in which cultures were civilized and primitive as colonialism advanced. Some cultures still lived a Paleolithic lifestyle while others had technologies that were current to that time. These were the differences that interested cultural anthropologists.

Anthropology focuses on human lives in different regions of the world. Particularly, it focuses on their practices and beliefs. Ethnologists study and compare the relationships between different cultures and their various characteristics. Ethnology is separated into two groups, one of which believed that cultures that were similar "somehow" learned from one another. Grafton Elliot Smith was a leading member of those that surmised that these different groups went through the same or similar stages of cultural evolution. It was also known as classical social evolutionism, of which Lewis Henry Morgan was a staunch advocate.

Franz Boas (1858–1942) went against Morgan's analysis that societies/cultures could be classified on a scale ranging from savagery and barbarism to civilization.

Franz Boas was influenced by German tradition. He argued that there were distinct cultures, not societies, that could be measured in the amount of civilization they had acquired compared to European standards. He believed that each culture had to be studied in its entirety and argued that cross-cultural generations were not possible. Instead, human behavior and conduct resulted from nurture, not nature. This belief was the result of his study on immigrant children. This scientific view of anthropology led to Boas and his fight against discrimination for immigrants, blacks, and indigenous American peoples. Several anthropologists went on to adopt his practices that are still relevant today. One example of Boasian anthropology is the "four-field approach" that is divided into sociocultural, biological, linguistic, and archaeology. The main emphasis for the four fields is culture.

Among the anthropologists that followed Franz Boas' principles was Edward Sapir and Ruth Benedict. As students of Boas, they were among many that provided details that attacked the theory of a single evolutionary process. Their studies of indigenous North

American cultures helped to cement linguistics as a general science and evolve it from its primary focus on Indo-European languages.

Linguistics

Linguistic anthropology studies how language influences a culture's social life. This branch of anthropology began as an effort to document languages that were becoming extinct and now covers almost all aspects of language structure and use.

What is known today as linguistic anthropology evolved from three unique concepts. The first was anthropological linguistics, which focuses on documenting disappearing languages, primarily in Native Americans. Edward Sapir was one of the leading founders of anthropological linguistics and is well known for his classification schemes of indigenous languages of the Americas.

The second concept is linguistic anthropology and the switch in the name signified a change in the study focus. The new term was most often used by Dell Hymes, whose vision for the future of linguistics included studying the language in its context. This is also when anthropologists began using mechanical recordings to preserve and later study the languages.

The third concept was developed in the late 1980s. Video documentation of cultural languages was being used to support research. Instead of only focusing on the language, anthropologists were studying the culture using linguistic tools that included investigating personal and social identities within the culture, shared ideologies, and constructing spoken interactions with individuals in the culture.

It was through Sapir's and other linguistic anthropologists' work that anthropology began addressing how language can be a cultural influence.

Archaeology

In Europe, archaeology or archeology, is either its own discipline or a sub-field of another. In North America, it is a sub-field of anthropology. Archaeology is the study of human activity, by recovering and analyzing the culture's materials. This includes artifacts, eco/biofacts, architecture, and cultural landscapes.

Archaeologists study human prehistory and history. It is distinct from paleontology, which studies fossil remains. For example, an archaeologist would be the one to study the stone tools discovered at Lomekwi in East Africa that date back approximately 3.3 million years ago.

The term archaeologist was first cited by the Oxford English Dictionary in 1824. Previously, the discipline was referred to as antiquarianism. Referred to as antiquarians, they studied ancient artifacts, historical sites, and manuscripts. One of the first recorded major archaeological excavations was at Stonehenge by John Aubrey (1626–1697), along with other megalithic sites in southern England. He was one of the first to attempt to chronologically chart the evolution of handwriting, costumes, medieval architecture, and shield shapes.

William Cunnington (1754–1810) is often called the "father of archaeological excavations." The terms he used to categorize and describe the Neolithic and Bronze Age barrows are still in use today. Since the purpose of archaeology is to learn about past cultures and the development of the human race, set applications are used in a specific order. Remote sensing helps to locate sites, while also providing information about the surrounding area. Next, a field survey is conducted to locate areas of specific interest. Once the site has been surveyed, careful excavation begins. The final application is to analyze the findings.

It was through the study of archaeology that the first stone tools, referred to as Oldowan, which were in use till approximately 1.7 million years ago, were discovered. Due to the lack of written records during human prehistory, archaeologists also discovered one stage of human evolution during the Paleolithic period, when hominins evolved into australopithecines in Africa.

 Applied Anthropology

John van Willigen and Satish Kedia, in their book Applied Anthropology: Domains of Application, wrote that applied anthropology is a "complex of related, research-based, instrumental methods which produce change or stability in specific cultural systems through the provision of data, initiation of direct action, and/or the formulation of policy."

Applied anthropology uses the methods and theory of anthropology to analyze and find solutions to practical problems. This field applies both researcher involvement and activism within the studied community.

In some sense, almost all anthropologists can be considered a part of the applied anthropology field. It is the culmination, in a sense, of all four sub-sets. One example of applied anthropology being used by all four sub-sets is working with a Native American community development program. Archaeological evidence can be used to determine claims on water rights. Ethnography can assess past and current cultural aspects of the community. Linguistics help to ensure the language is passed down to younger generations, and anthropology can determine and track diseases that might be caused by a dietary deficiency. All of this information, past and present, can help the culture decide how best to go on in the future.

Applied anthropologists are often employed by nonacademic clients. This can include development agencies, advocacy groups, and tribal/ethnic organizations, along with government and non-governmental groups and businesses. Often, the applied anthropologists use their methods to help inform policy makers and/or market products. Some of their methodology tools include ethnography, participant observations, interviews, and focus groups.

There can also be a moral dilemma that applied anthropologists can face from nonacademic clients, which was noted by van Willigen and Kedia: "The ethical requirements of applied anthropology are especially challenging since the practitioner must negotiate an intricate balance between the interests of the clients who commission the work, and those of the community being studied." Applied anthropologists must be sensitive to the community's needs and culturally sensitive when they're conducting their research. There are ethical guidelines in place that applied anthropologists are expected to follow. However, it is getting more difficult. For example, the cutting of female genitalia is "normal" in some cultures, while others find the practice barbaric. Anthropologists that write about the practice in a culturally sensitive and professional tone are often criticized for supporting it.

In the United States, there are three primary groups that are based on applied anthropology and closely follow and pay attention to ethics and the social implications of their research. They are the American Anthropological Association (AAA), the National Association for the Practice of Anthropology (NAPA), and the Society for Applied Anthropology (SFAA).

HISTORY AND THEORY

Ethnographies and Perspectives

Ethnology, or cultural anthropology, is the study of an identifiable group of people, and the writings by researchers are referred to as ethnographies. The word ethnography is derived from the Greek words "ethnos" for people and "graphein" for writing. Ethnographies help to put the findings from fieldwork, surveys, and interviews into a format that is easy for laymen to read and understand.

While ethnographies can take several forms, including journals, articles, statistical data, and documentaries, almost all reflect the anthropologist's desire to convey holism. Holism is the idea shared by many cultural anthropologists, including the founder of American anthropology Franz Boas, that the idea of the culture as a whole is greater than its individual parts. This means a single individual that might have accomplished great things is not more important than the culture as a whole. The perspective cannot be solely based on individuals.

Ethnographies, or a type of one, can be dated as far back as the second century BCE. Zhang Qian (164–113 BCE) spent over twenty-five years traveling through Central Asia, as far as Uzbekistan, on orders from Emperor Wu of the Han Dynasty to record the cultures and peoples of Central Asia. Not only did the information gathered help open new trade routes along the Silk Road, it also introduced Buddhism into Chinese culture.

Ethnographies and the perspectives they provide have challenged commonly held beliefs from Sir Charles Lyell (1797–1875) that observed the layers of rock and argued that the surface of the earth must have changed over extended periods of time. This went against the "young earth theory" that was supported by biblical information that dated the earth at only six thousand years old.

The documented research also helped dispel some beliefs that were held by anthropologists that all societies go through the same stages of development. This led to the now widely held belief that cultures differ but this does not make one more advanced than another. This is referred to as cultural relativism, developed by Franz Boas.

 ## Sex and Gender

Anthropologists in several sub-fields, primarily cultural and biological, observe the characteristics that define sex and gender in a society. The goal is to understand human sex differences in relation to gender, while also accepting that cultural beliefs and expectations play a significant role. These beliefs and expectations in the society can affect everything from their assigned activities to their living spaces and how they're fed. As with eunuchs (a third sex role), anthropologists also have to accept that there is another sex role, other than masculine and feminine.

Gender roles are an important part of anthropological study. These roles can vary in different cultures. While an individual's sex is simple to determine, their gender role cannot be based on one specific theory. In the early twentieth century, it was still widely presumed among anthropologists that the political and social differences/divisions between men and women were natural, meaning the same in every culture.

It wasn't until anthropologist Phyllis Kaberry's fieldwork in the 1930s with Australian Aborigines that ethnographies depicted women as "active agents." However, she went on to reveal that while women weren't necessarily subservient, they were below men in politics. Margaret Mead, a former student of Franz Boas, demonstrated that the ideals of masculine and feminine characteristics vary tremendously throughout different cultures. This belief is still held today.

Anthropologists look to examine which aspects of social relations in a culture have a greater impact than others. For example, in the 1970s, young women began questioning their gender roles, and this became apparent in fieldwork and literature. This also raised additional questions about the anthropological theory that some gender characteristics are formed by nature.

 ## Race and Ethnicity

Ethnicity is broadly defined as "the cultural characteristics that connect a particular group or groups of people to each other." This was the simple definition before the twenty-first century. As previously mentioned, race is defined by specific physical characteristics, like facial features or skin color, while ethnicity was used to describe the culture and region the group is from.

Today, anthropologists are finding it much harder to accept these simple definitions. Instead, they are more likely to demand accounts of the particular formation of an ethnic identity in a specific place and time. Anthropologists look beyond racial characteristics;

they see ethnicity as natural or expected correspondence between physical features, behaviors, and attitudes.

The terms "race" and "ethnicity" did not become commonly used until the mid-nineteenth century. Employed by pre- and post-Darwin scholars, it was later used by anthropologists to discuss human racial and cultural classifications. Social/cultural anthropologists did not begin using ethnicity as a unique term until the 1950s. Throughout the nineteenth and part of the twentieth century, race was the dominant term/concept used to describe the scientific, political, and social/cultural classification of human groups in the Western world.

The eighteenth century saw the start of "enlightenment," which in turn helped to begin the specific scientific classifications of humans, particularly those of non-European and "colonized" cultures. Before the scientific community accepted Darwin's "theory of evolution," humans were thought to be the product of a divine being or intervention. Monogenists closely followed the biblical creation story of Adam and Eve and believed that all people, and subsequently races, derived from this single creation. Polygenists, however, believed that there was a separate creation for each of the major races. Both proponents of these pre-evolutionary models used continental labels for creating the physical races. Anthropologists presumed that all Europeans, Native Americans, Asians, and Africans were naturally distinct from each other, even on the level of species (i.e., one race might be more advanced than another).

Even with the acceptance of Darwin's evolutionary theory, anthropologists were still trying to fix their ideas of race and racial connections to a culture's ethnic identity. Morphology (the study of an organism/human and its structure) was used to quantify human variation, although most commonly it compared skull size and shape, often erroneously. These practices were the basis for the methodology developed in physical anthropology for Europe and the United States.

Based on this mislabeled or false anthropometric data, physical anthropologists wrongly labeled cultures "nonwhite" as being less evolved. The evolutionary ideas that were used initially in global classifications, also classified people on behavioral, cultural, and physical scales. These physical anthropologists also considered Caucasian women, European and Euro-American people of lower socio-economic class, convicted criminals, individuals with disabilities, and anyone that practiced scandalous sexual practices (e.g., prostitution, adultery, and homosexuality) to be lower on the natural scale of evolution.

These same misconceptions also believed that non-Caucasians were more susceptible to various cultural and behavioral vices by nature. This meant that they were also less developed than Caucasians. This erroneous labeling of non-Caucasian cultures has led to the stereotypes that still exist today in the form of racism and cultural isolationism.

When the term "ethnicity" took on new meaning in the 1960s and 1970s, it was used to describe a more fluid cultural process of identity formation. Up until then, it was still used to describe a fixed person (their race). The term ethnic started to mean, in the United States and globally, "someone not from my country." It demarked an individual as being lower-class. Ideas regarding race and ethnicity were easily interchangeable until the mid-1970s.

Franz Boas was one of the first and possibly most influential cultural anthropologists, and his 1912 study of cranial plasticity in American immigrants contested the theory for the fixed physical nature of ethnic and racial identity. While Boas first began questioning the long-held theory on race and ethnicity, it was the rise of Nazism and Aryan "pride" that the greater anthropology and social sciences as a whole recognized that racism applied to the terms and the organization as a whole.

The major change was adding "group" to the term "ethnic." Tribe and tribalism, particularly used to describe African cultures, was replaced with "ethnic group." Modern anthropologists hope that the use of these two terms will help dispel the racial bigotry that still exists today.

Cultural Ecology and Evolution

Anthropologist Charles O. Frake, in 1962, described cultural ecology as "the study of the role of culture as a dynamic component of any ecosystem." An estimated one-third to one-half of the earth's land surface has been affected or transformed by human development. Cultural ecology argues that humans have been inextricably embedded in earth surface processes (building, farming, herding, etc.) centuries before man invented tools such as bulldozers and dynamite.

Key Cultural Ecology Points

- The term cultural ecology was first used by the American anthropologist Julian Steward in the 1950s.
- Cultural ecology theorizes that humans are part of their environment and both equally affect and are affected by the other.
- Modern cultural ecology combines elements of political and historical ecology, along with post-modernism, theory or rational choice, and cultural materialism.

Cultural ecology, as developed by Stewart, recognized that the ecological location plays a significant role in shaping the region's cultures. The method Stewart used was separated into three steps:

1. Document methods and technologies that are used to get a living (make money) from the environment.

2. Study the patterns of human behavior/culture associated with the use of the environment.

3. Assess how much these behavioral patterns influence other cultural aspects. For example, a region that receives little rainfall may develop patterns where concerns over water permeates every aspect of the culture's life. This can lead to the creation of a religious belief system that is centered around water and rainfall. However, a culture that lives in a region that receives adequate rainfall would probably not have the same religious belief system.

Cultural ecology is a major subfield of anthropology and is derived from Franz Boas' work. Throughout the twentieth century and into the twenty-first, it has continued to follow Stewart's theory and has branched out to cover additional aspects of human society (i.e., distribution of wealth and power in a society and how this affects behaviors such as hoarding or gifting). One example of fieldwork that studied gifting, or potlatch, was done along the American and Canadian Pacific Northwest Coast.

The indigenous peoples of that region referred to the practice of leaders having a gift-giving feast as a potlatch. During the feast, the leader will either give away or destroy valuable items as a symbol of wealth and power. This is in direct contrast to how Western cultures view wealth and power, where it is to be amassed, not given away.

While cultural ecology studies the environment and the effect it has on people and vice versa, cultural evolution is the theory of social change. There have been theories about cultural evolution since Aristotle proposed that the development of cultural form automatically ceased once maturity was reached. For example, poetry had developed as far as it could go and would remain basically the same.

Early cultural evolutionists often subscribed to Darwin's theory of evolution—both variation and selective inheritance contributed to human evolution and gave mankind the capacity to acquire language. By the early twentieth century and especially following WWI, "evolution" was being shunned, along with other "Darwinian" ideas. This was also brought about by the rediscovery of Mendelian genetics—in which genes come in pairs. Gregor Mendel is considered the "father of genetics."

By the 1950s, metaphors once used by cultural evolutionists were slowly being revived. Donald T. Campbell's work in 1960 was one of the catalysts for this. Campbell drew on the work by American geneticist, Sewall Wright, to draw a parallel between genetic evolution, variance, and selective retention of creative ideas. This evolved into the full theory of socio-cultural evolution in 1965. Campbell stated that "cultural evolution was not an analogy from organic evolution per se, but rather from a general model for quasi-teleological processes for which organic evolution is but one instance."

In 1975, anthropologist F. T. Cloak argued for the existence of learnt cultural instructions resulting in material artifacts, e.g., the wheel. This introduced the argument of whether cultural evolution requires neurological instructions.

Beginning in the nineteenth century, cultural evolution has given rise to several theories. These include:

- Unilinear theory, developed in the nineteenth century, which proposed that all societies and cultures develop on the same path. Herbert Spencer was among the first to present this theory. In 1877, Lewis H. Morgan published Ancient Society, in which he lists seven stages of human culture:

    1. lower, middle, and upper savagery
    2. lower, middle, and upper barbarism
    3. civilization

- Cultural particularism, in which, in the late nineteenth century, it was mistakenly believed (and thought to be racist by some) that all culture was borne out of Western Europe and the United States. Anthropologist Franz Boas changed this unilinear belief to cultural particularism, in which the emphasis shifted to a multilinear approach concerning cultural evolution. With this approach, cultures were now assessed separately instead of being compared to each other.

- Multilinear theory, the introduction of which revived the debate on cultural evolution that proposed there were no fixed stages toward cultural development. Instead, there are several stages of varying lengths and forms. Even though the theory states that cultures develop differently, along with cultural evolution, all societies do tend to develop and advance over time.

- Dual inheritance theory, which is also referred to as biocultural evolution, or gene-culture coevolution, the dual inheritance theory was developed throughout the 1960s until the 1980s. It proposes that human behavior is the product of two different and interacting evolutionary processes: cultural and gene evolution. The theory states that genes and culture are continuously interacting. Changes in genes can affect culture and vice versa. One of the theory's central claims is that culture partly evolves through a Darwinian selection process, or what dual inheritance theorists describe as "genetic evolution."

- Memetics gained some attention with the 1976 book The Selfish Gene by evolutionary biologist Richard Dawkins. A meme is an idea-replicator that can reproduce by jumping from one human mind to another. It was represented as a "virus of the mind" image and thought to be a "unit of culture," e.g., a belief, idea, pattern of behavior, etc. The variations and selection in the replication process allows for Darwinian evolution and makes memetics a mechanism of cultural evolution. This theory tries to account for certain cultural traits, like terrorist suicide. They successfully spread the meme for martyrdom but were fatal to themselves and other people. This is why memes are often seen as selfish and only interested in their success.

- Evolutionary epistemology, which refers to a theory that applies biological evolutionary concepts to the growth of human knowledge. It argues that parts of knowledge evolve according to selection, particularly scientific theories. This is a naturalistic approach to epistemology. It emphasizes the importance of natural selection in two main roles:

1. Selection is the generator and the maintainer of the reliability of our cognitive movements and senses.
2. Selection processes are thought to be the evolution of scientific theory through trial and error.

Evolutionary epistemologists believe that all theories are only provisionally true, regardless of the degree of empirical testing that might state it to be correct.

PHYSICAL ANTHROPOLOGY

 Genetic Principles

By the early 1900s, fundamental principles of genetic inheritance had been established and anthropologists began using the same principles and new empirical data to bring attention to the long-standing problems associated with human variation and primate phylogeny. Scientists first focused on characteristics in human blood. Geneticists quantified the regional differences in an ABO genotype. They then tried to correlate the differences with more traditional assessments of variation.

Anthropologists were interested in alleles, such as the sickling trait that had adaptive significance. After blood samples were available from other primates in the mid twentieth century, it was possible to create phylogenetic trees based on genetic data. These "trees" were then compared to results from the fossil record.

After the end of WWII, it was possible for anthropologists to collect blood samples from global cultures. These field expeditions were organized by anthropological geneticists. Not only did researchers collect human samples, but they also gathered cultural and linguist data. The goal was finding correlations that could detect evolutionary trends and reconstruct human migration. In the 1980s, all four anthropology fields became intertwined with genetics research, both individually and in cross-disciplinary research. The research agenda anthropological geneticists use is a four-step process:

1. human origins
2. prehistoric migration
3. coevolution of biology, culture, and language
4. variation and adaption to modern environments

The fields of anthropology and genetics have not always coexisted peacefully. The eugenics movement in the 1920s promoted selective breeding to either remove negative traits or increase the likelihood of positive ones. Since most of the perceived "negative" traits primarily existed in minority, uneducated, and lower-income populations, it was viewed as racist by many anthropologists and lost popularity over the years. In the 1990s, it was genetic essentialism that the two debated. Genetic essentialism is defined as the tendency to presume that an individual's behaviors and characteristics are based on their perceived genetic makeup.

In an effort to stress how the two scientific fields complement each other, human genetics became the foundation for the study of human microevolution. The primary data would be biochemical makers of ancestry or intergenerational continuity. In anthropology, genetic research asks four types of questions:

1. patterns of human variation
2. phylogenetic (evolutionary) relationship among humans and primate species
3. the migration and adaptation of human populations (microevolution)
4. relationships among biological variation and other kinds of human variation, e.g., language and culture

Human Variation

After WWII, human genetics become more focused on real genetically-based medical pathologies (e.g., sickle cell anemia) instead of perceived ones such as "feeblemindedness." This research made it clear that the simple rules of the Mendelian inheritance theory only applied to the inheritance of biochemical variants and pathological conditions.

The interesting physical characteristics of human variation, such as complexion, facial and hair form, height, and body build, etc. were the result of more complex developmental and hereditary physiologies that involve the coordinated activities of several genes, along with their relation to specific environmental, cultural, and genetic contexts.

The main theoretical model that emerged to describe human genetic variation during the twentieth century was the cline. This is the gradual geographic change in the frequency of an allele. Anthropologists surmised the physical form and genetic variation seemed to differ across human species in a continuous, quantitative fashion.

Adaption

One of the strongest examples of human genetic adaptation was presented by Frank B. Livingstone in 1958. His study of the sickle cell disease, primarily in Africa, presented convincing evidence that sickle blood cells were the genetic response to the presence of malaria.

His work went on to illustrate other lessons in genetic anthropology. It showed that the heterozygote (individual with two different alleles for a specific gene) or a carrier of hemoglobin S (HbS) had an adaptive advantage, not someone with two identical alleles for a specific gene or homozygote that suffered from sickle cell anemia. It also showed that sickle cell anemia was a successful genetic solution to a mostly man-made problem: malaria spread by mosquitoes, which were attracted to standing water that also started early agricultural practices.

This is the most firmly established correlation between genetic variations and pathological diseases. Two other examples are porphyria variegate among the South African Boers and Ellis-van Creveld syndrome in the Pennsylvania Amish. Both diseases were elevated in these populations due to a seventeenth-century immigrant that was a carrier of the genetic disease and an ancestor of the modern populations. Most other diseases that can be associated with genetic variants show extremely ambiguous patterns.

Population Genetics

When funding increased after WWII, anthropologists returned to researching isolated small-scale populations, and a biological anthropologist was often a member of the team. One of the most noted of these joint research operations occurred in the 1960s. Led by James Neel, his team conducted an intensive study of the Yanomamö, an indigenous people that lived in the upper drainage of the Orinoco River in Brazil and Venezuela.

Genetic research included examining blood systems that were known at the time with seven Yanomamö villages, seven Makiritare villages—a nearby tribe—and twelve other tribes in Central and South America. After comparing the groups, researchers concluded that human evolution might have been preceding at a pace one hundred times faster than previously believed. This is if these small scale societies can be taken as an analog of earlier Pleistocene or Paleolithic humans.

These studies on human genetics eventually did not provide insight into the mechanics of human evolution. By 1974, Henry Harpending had concluded that these studies, "…have not advanced our understanding of human evolution in a global sense." He went on to state that "…the sample sizes were too small to allow for reliable inferences about natural selection."

Evolution of Primates

By the 1920s, it was established that human blood was more similar to that of chimpanzees than horses were to donkeys. Allan Wilson and Vincent Sarich demonstrated in 1967 that since biochemical variation distinguishable immunologically tends to track the time, it is possible to tell when certain species diverged from each other.

While we now know a lot about human similarities with chimpanzees genetically, we still don't know genetically what makes us different, like language, bipedality, cooperative breeding, evaporative heat loss, and other significant ways humans differ from primates.

Modern studies of primate genetics looks at divergent times and systematics, but also paternity, demography, conservation, and microevolution.

Evolutionary Principles

Evolutionary principles are often used in medicine and agriculture. Examples of these would be:

- slowing the resistances that weeds, pests, and pathogens can develop through evolution
- breeding programs designed for maximum crop yield or higher quality

- natural resource management
- environmental science
- conservation biology

Some other examples include protecting isolated or small populations from inbreeding depression, identifying key traits that occur in adapting to climate change, and the design of harvesting regimes that minimize unwanted life-history evolution, to name a few.

While the various fields incorporate evolutionary principles in their work, there are four key themes that all follow. These are:

1. variation
2. selection
3. connectivity
4. eco-evolutionary dynamics

 Variation

Variation (phenotypic) determines how organisms interact with their environment and respond to the pressures that result from selection. A variation can come from several forms, such as:

- genetic differences
- the potential for an organism to produce different phenotypes in varying environments (individual phenotypic plasticity)
- gene expression regulated by DNA (epigenetic changes)
- influence of the mother's phenotype on that of her offspring
- other forms of nongenetic inheritance

By understanding the origins, nature, and maintenance of this variation, researchers are provided an important foundation that can help them predict and interpret responses to changing environmental conditions.

Selection

Natural selection is the force that changes variation into evolutionary changes. Selection happens when a certain pheno/genotype has a higher degree of "fitness" than another. In populations that are well-adapted, there may be limited selection since most individuals are near their environmental fitness peak. However, this is expected to change for all populations. As the environment changes, humans become maladapted. Understanding selection can help scientists better understand how environmental changes affect a populace. This is information that is being used as the world climate continues to change.

Connectivity

The movement of individuals and gametes across an environment is determined by connectivity. There are several factors that can influence connectivity:

- behavior and body size
- population densities/distributions
- man-made structures such as dams, roads, canals, corridors, etc.
- nature-made structures such as oceans, seas, lakes, rivers, mountains, canyons, etc.

Ecologically, increased connectivity can be positive (demographic rescue) but it can also be negative (invasive species spread diseases). Genetically, gene flow increase can boost genetic variation within populations (bringing new genes to the gene pool). However, it can also decrease genetic variation by mixing the different gene pools. This can either enhance or constrain an adaptive evolution.

Eco-Evolutionary Dynamics

Variation, selection, and connectivity are all considered in eco-evolutionary dynamics as scientists look to see how each influences the evolution of phenotypic traits. This is done to see how evolution could affect population dynamics. These dynamics are covered under ecology and evolution and how the two interact with each other.
The second part of eco-evolutionary dynamics examines the effects of phenotypic/genetic change on the make-up of a population. These effects can include:

- the number of individuals
- population persistence
- community structure (diversity of species)
- ecosystem function, the cycling of nutrients, decomposition, and primary productivity

These dynamics can be used to study human and animal species.

Primatology

Primatology is the scientific study of primates. It's the boundary between mammalogy and anthropology. Primatologists study extinct and living primates in labs and their natural habits by conducting experiments and fieldwork in an effort to understand their evolution and behavior. There are two main primatology centers: Western and Japanese. Their areas of research and data obtaining methods are different, but they do share many of the same principles.

Western Primatology

The origins of Western primatology are primarily European and North American. Early studies on primates focused mainly on medical research, but there were scientists conducting experiments to determine primate intelligence and the limits of their cognitive power.

The theory of Western primatology focuses on the common links between primates and humans. It studies the psychological and biological aspects of primates. It is thought that through understanding human's closest animal relatives, it might be possible to understand the nature of primate's and human's share.

There are three methodologies for primatology:

1. the "realistic" approach through a field study,
2. the "controlled" approach conducted in a lab, and
3. the "semi-free ranging" approach in which habit and social structure is replicated in a controlled environment.

All types of primate studies are designed to be neutral/unbiased. While subjective research is done, the emphasis in Western primatology is the objective of the study. Some notable Western primatologists include Dian Fossey, whose work at the Karisoke Research Center in Rwanda proved that habituation was a possibility among mountain gorillas. Jane Goodall's studies of chimpanzees in Tanzania used simple tools, such as twigs, to dig into a termite nest.

Japanese Primatology

The origins of Japanese primatology came from animal ecology. Its formation is accredited to Kinji Imanishi, an animal ecologist that began studying wild horses before concentrating on primate ecology. In 1950, he help start the Primate Research Group. The additional founder of Japanese primatology was Junichiro Itani. He was a famous anthropologist and professor at Kyoto University. He was the co-founder of the Primate Research Group and the Center for African Area Studies.

The Japanese primatology theory is often more interested in the social aspects of primates. Anthropology and social evolution are a primary focus for Japanese researchers. They believe that by studying primates, they'll gain insight into the dual human nature—individual self versus social self.

Japanese primatology is extremely disciplined and it is also a subjective science. It is thought that the best data only comes through identifying with your subject. Instead of neutrality, it is a more casual research environment. Researcher and subject are often allowed to mingle freely. It is not only desirable to domesticate nature, but it is also necessary for study.

Primatology in Sociobiology

Sociobiology looks to understand all animal species in the context of their advantageous and disadvantageous behavior, while primatology only studies human and non-human primates. Where these two fields meet is examining the evolutionary details of primate behavioral processes. This is done to help understand human evolution and behavior.

While the father of taxonomy, Carl Linnaeus, first organized natural objects into what is now referred to as "evolutionary readiness," and Darwin later developed his theory of evolution, it wasn't until the 1900s that it was proven that humans and simians share a majority of DNA. Humans and chimpanzees share 97–99 percent genetic identity.

Researchers also look at social behavior, like grooming, as a form of language. It is an intense bonding experience between two primates, and indicates a strong troop alliance. British anthropologist Robin Dunbar suggested that there could be a link between primate grooming and the development of human language. As the troop grows larger, it becomes impossible for chimpanzees to individually groom everyone, which could lead to a need for a new form of communication/language.

It was also noted that primates have dominance hierarchies. The main function is to maintain stability within the troop by having dominant and submissive members.

Paleontology

Paleontology is the scientific study of life that existed before, and occasionally, during the Holocene Epoch—which occurred approximately 11,700 years before the present. This is the current geological epoch that began after the last glacial period. An epoch is a specific period of time marked by notable events or particular characteristics.

This science, including the study of fossils and observations pertaining to paleontology, has been found dating back to the fifth century BCE. In the eighteenth century, it became established as a science due to Georges Cuvier's work on comparative anatomy. The term paleontology originates from three Greek words: palaios (ancient), ontos (being or creature), and logos (thought or study).
In simple terms, paleontology is the study of ancient life. It looks for information about past organisms that include:

- identity and origin,
- environment and evolution, and
- information about earth's inorganic and organic past.

Paleontology was classified as a historical science by William Whewell (1794–1866). Since it tries to describe past events and reconstruct the causes, there are three elements to paleontology research. These are:

1. describing past events,
2. developing a general theory to explain the reasons for the different types of changes, and
3. applying the theories to specific facts.

Paleontologists usually come up with multiple theories to explain an event and then look for the evidence that supports one. Sometimes the evidence discovery is by luck and not research. A good example of this is the discovery of iridium, primarily an extraterrestrial metal, in 1980 by Luis and Walter Alvarez. The metal was discovered in the Cretaceous-Tertiary boundary layer in the earth's soil that was made by an asteroid impact. This helped support the popular theory for the extinction that took place during the Cretaceous-Paleogene event, roughly sixty-six million years ago.

Paleontology, as a science, is between geology and biology. It focuses on past life (biology) but its primary source of evidence are fossils (geology). Paleontologists also work with archaeologists. Paleontologists can identify plant and animal fossils discovered at a dig site.

The science also has several subdivisions that include:
- Vertebrate paleontology, which focuses on fossils from the earliest known fish (Entelognathus primordialis) approximately 419 million years ago in China.
- Invertebrate paleontology, which focuses on fossils like arthropods, mollusks, annelid worms, and echinoderms. Invertebrates are some of the oldest animals on earth. The oldest fossil discovered, so far, is a trilobite that evolved during the Cambrian Period approximately 500 million years ago.
- Paleobotany, which focuses on fossil plants, algae, and fungi. These fossils are used to study the evolution of plant life. One of the oldest plant fossils found dates approximately 72 to 79 million years ago and is the earliest record of the mahogany family. Found on Vancouver Island, Canada, mahogany is used to understand rainforest evolution.
- Palynology, which focuses on pollen and spores produced by land plants and protists. It is between botany and paleontology since it studies living and fossilized organisms. The earliest recorded observations of pollen under a microscope date to English botanist Nehemiah Grew in the 1640s.
- Micropaleontology, which focuses on microscopic fossil organisms of all types.

Fossils are usually the most informative evidence from a specific period, but the record is incomplete, especially farther back in time. This is because not only is fossilization a rare occurrence, but erosion and metamorphism can destroy the fossils before they're discovered. This is true for all three groups of fossils: bones, shells, and wood.

Paleontologists also study trace fossils. These are mainly burrows and tracks that sometimes contain fossilized feces (coprolites) and other indications of feeding in the area. This type of fossil not only provides a source of data that is unique to the animals, but also reflects behavioral patterns. The earliest trace fossils, excluding stromatolites, date from 2,000 to 1,800 million years ago.

Geochemical observation can help narrow down a specific period of time for a biological activity. For example, the geochemical features of rocks might be able to reveal when life first began on earth. Currently, it is thought that the first signs of life began approximately 3.5 billion years ago. This date is supported by undisputed scientific evidence, but there is some evidence emerging that suggests life started as early as 4.5 billion years ago.

Classifying ancient organisms is important to prevent confusion and disputes. Linnaean taxonomy is the most common method used but there are difficulties when new organisms are discovered that are different from the existing known ones.

Dating organisms involves seeing how living creatures have evolved over time. One problem is estimating fossil dates. Beds, where fossils are often found, are not conducive to radiometric dating due to the missing elements. This is also the only technique currently approved and available at dating rocks older than 50 million years with any accuracy of 0.5 percent or higher.

The principle behind radiometric dating is simple. It uses the known rates at which various radioactive elements decay. This rate of decay is used to date certain fossils found in rocks of a volcanic origin. Only fossil-bearing rocks found in volcanic ash layers can be dated radiometrically.

When radiometric dating isn't possible, paleontologists turn to stratigraphy. This is the science of deciphering the sedimentary record. Since rocks typically form horizontal layers with the youngest being on top, fossils found in or between the layers can be approximately dated if the period the sediment was formed is known.

History of Life

It is a scientific fact that the earth was formed approximately 4.5 billion years ago and the collision that formed the moon was roughly 40 million years later. Some theories suggest that at this time, the earth could have cooled enough to allow oceans and an atmosphere to form. There is evidence that a Late Heavy Bombardment of asteroids struck the moon 4.1 to 3.8 billion years ago and, if the earth was also hit, the first oceans and atmosphere could've been stripped away.

Paleontology traces evolutionary history of life back 3,000 million years and possibly as far as 3.8 million years ago. Substantiated evidence dates life back 3 million years but new data is possibly showing that there is fossil bacteria from 3.4 million years ago, along with geochemical evidence of life as far back as 3,800 million years ago. Even though there is a group of scientists researching the theory that life was "seeded" on it—came from microorganisms on an asteroid—most studies focus on how life started and evolved on Earth.

Scientists know that microbial mats—layered colonies of bacteria—were the dominant species on earth for roughly 2,000 million years. From here, multicell life developed around 2.1 million years ago. The earliest evidence of multicell life is the Francevillian Group fossils dating back 2.1 million years. However, specialization of cells for various functions first appeared 1,430 million years ago—possibly fungus—and a possible red alga 1,200 million years ago.

It is thought that specialization only occurs with sexual reproduction. Asexual multicell organisms might be at risk of being overrun with rogue cells that have the ability to reproduce.

Cnidarians are the earliest known animals from around 580 million years ago. Found in fresh and marine environments, it is theorized that these might be descendants of even earlier animals due to their "modern" appearance. The earliest bilaterian animals that resemble some species today can be dated back to the early Cambrian, approximately 541 million years ago.

What is referred to as the CambrianExplosion occurred around that time. This was when a rapid evolutionary advancement occurred, resulting in several species or "weird wonders" due to their limited resemblance to known animals. Some paleontologists believe that modern appearing animals evolved earlier and their fossils just haven't been discovered yet. Another theory is that the "weird wonders" are what is known as evolutionary "aunts and cousins" of modern animal groups.

Organisms needed evolution to move from water to land. This includes plants and animals. Support against gravity and protection from dehydration were some of the problems evolution needed to solve. This seems to have occurred around 476 million years ago for plants and 490 million years ago for invertebrates.

The Permian Period (298.9 million years ago) was possibly when the ancestors of mammals, or synapsids, dominated land areas. However, the Permian-Triassic extinction event (251 million years ago) came close to ending complex life. During the recovery, a new group became dominant. Archosaurs were the most diverse and abundant vertebrates on land. One group, dinosaurs, were the dominant land vertebrates for the remainder of the Mesozoic Period (252 to 66 million years ago).

The Cretaceous-Paleogene extinction event wiped out most of the dinosaurs 66 million years ago, except for birds. After the event, mammals began increasing quickly in diversity and size, with some taking to the air, sea, or staying on land.

Over 6 million years ago, the earliest fossil evidence of human ancestors, upright walking primates, was discovered. Fossil evidence also suggests that brain size in humans began increasing roughly 3 million years ago. There is an ongoing debate among paleontologists over whether humans descended from a small population in Africa that migrated over the world less than 200,000 years ago and replaced previous hominin species or evolved simultaneously worldwide as the result of interbreeding.

ARCHAEOLOGY

Methodology

Starting in the 1860s up to the turn of the century, the five basic methods of archaeology were created. These are the

1. stratigraphic excavation
2. significance of a small find and plain artifact
3. copious use of field notes, plan maps, and photography to record the excavation process
4. publication of the results
5. beginnings of a cooperative excavation and indigenous rights to archaeological finds

Stratigraphic Methods

Also referred to as the "big dig," stratigraphic excavation is the careful removal of each layer of dirt at an archaeological site. Italian archaeologist Giuseppe Fiorelli (1823–1896) was one of the first to start tracking stratigraphic layers during the excavations at Pompeii in 1860. This helped to preserve many of the site's features. Fiorelli believed that artifacts and art were secondary to what he thought was the primary reason for a dig—to learn about the city or site and all of the inhabitants. To pass along his disciplines, he opened an archaeological school for both Italians and foreigners.

Fiorelli isn't known as the father of the "big dig," only for creating some of the archaeological methods used today. German archaeologist Ernst Curtius (1814–1896) has this distinction with his 1875 excavation at Olympia. He was also one of the first to give indigenous rights to Greece for any archaeological finds. Both Fiorelli and Curtius created copious amounts of notes and journals detailing every aspect of their digs, along with publications of their findings.

Scientific Methods

It was the work of three European archaeologists that produced the techniques and methodology of what is now known as "modern archaeology." Heinrich Schliemann (1822–1890) was often insultingly called a "treasure hunter" but by the time he was working on the excavation of Troy, he had been influenced by Curtius' methods at Olympus and began incorporating them into his work. By the end of his career, he was carefully recording his excavations, preserving ordinary artifacts, along with the extraordinary ones, and publishing reports in a timely manner.

The second European archaeologist of the trio of founders was Augustus Henry Lane-Fox Pitt-Rivers (1827–1910). He was a military man that brought military precision to his archaeological excavations. He also spent a large amount of his inheritance amassing an extensive comparative artifact collection, one of the first in the world.

Chronological Methods

The final member of the trio that helped found modern archaeology methods and techniques was William Matthew Flinders Petrie (1853–1942). He is best known for the invention of the dating technique used in excavation. Known as sequence or seriation dating, it is used to help plan out large digs. By using stratigraphic excavation and comparative artifact analysis, along with Egyptian dynastic information, he was able to synchronize the occupation levels at Tell el-Hesi. He was also able to successfully develop a complete and absolute chronology for sixty feet of debris left by the inhabitants.

Paleolithic and Mesolithic

The Paleolithic period coincides with the Pleistocene epoch, when geographical and climatic changes were occurring. Lasting from 2.6 million to approximately 12,000 years ago, this was an important time for humans in terms of development.

Humans were primarily located in eastern Africa, east of the Great Rift Valley. Most known fossils dating back over one million years ago have been found in this area that includes Ethiopia, Kenya, and Tanzania. At the start of the Paleolithic period, human population density is estimated at one person per square mile. Scientists speculate that the reason for the low population was due to a variety of factors that include:

- low body fat,
- a nomadic lifestyle,
- late infant weaning,
- infanticide, and
- women participating in the same grueling activities—hunting, gathering, and walking long distances.

It is thought that it wasn't until humans began settling down, primarily due to agriculture, that the population started to rise.

Distribution of Humans

Around 2,000,000–1,500,000 million years ago, small groups of hominins started leaving Africa to settle in southern Europe and Asia. By 1,700,000 BP, southern Caucasus was settled and northern China in 1,600,000 BP. At the end of the Lower Paleolithic, hominins were residing in China, Europe, western Indonesia, and around the Mediterranean. Fossil evidence shows that early hominins made it as far north as England, France, Bulgaria, and southern Germany. The lack of fossil evidence any further north during this period may be linked to a lack of fire control. Studies of caves settled in northern Europe do not show any signs of fire until around 400,000–300,000 BP.

Fossils discovered in east Asia are generally in the genus Homo erectus—thought to be the first humans to walk upright. Known lower Paleolithic sites in Europe have produced very little fossil evidence, but it is thought that these early settlers were also Homo erectus. While there is still debate about their relationship to modern humans, it is believed that there were at least two expansion events before people settled in Eurasia around 2,000,000–1,500,000 BP. At approximately 500,000 BP, it is thought that the first group of early humans (Homo heidelbergensis—of which there are four recognizable species) settled in Europe from Africa. This group eventually evolved into Homo neanderthalensis (Neanderthals). By the middle Paleolithic, Neanderthals had migrated to Poland.

By the end of the Paleolithic, both Homo erectus and Homo neanderthalensis were extinct. Modern Homo sapiens (descendants of Homo sapiens-sapiens) first appeared in the fossil record in eastern Africa around 200,000 BP. During this period, before other hominin species extinction, there's evidence that different groups co-existed together. There is also evidence of interbreeding between them through DNA.

Other hominin fossils have also been discovered in the Altai Mountains and Indonesia that do not belong to Homo sapiens or Homo neanderthalensis. These fossils have been radiocarbon dated to 30,000–40,000 BP (Altai Mountains) and 17,000 BP (Indonesia). There are a few facts to remember:

- One of the oldest hominid fossils found dates to 700,000 to 1,000,000 BCE. Discovered on the Island of Java, "Java Man" was discovered in 1891 or 1892.
- Between 1929 and 1937, fossils from Homo erectus were discovered near Beijing, China and known as the "Peking Man."
- As of now, the oldest known human fossils in the United States were discovered in Idaho dating back approximately 16,500 years ago.

 Tools

Paleolithic humans created tools made from bone, wood, and stone. Australopithecus—the ancestor of modern humans dating back 4.2 to 1.9 million years ago—are thought to be the first to use stone tools. This is based on excavations in Gona, Ethiopia, where thousands of artifacts have been found firmly dating back 2.6 million years.

The Oldowan is the earliest example of the stone tool style and dates back 2.6 million years ago. These tools were simply made, usually having one side chipped off to perform a specific task. Around 250,000 years ago, this was replaced by the Acheulean style. Slightly more complex, and conceived by Homo ergaster—an extinct chronospecies that existed 1.8 to 1.65 million years ago—these slightly more modern tools included rudimentary oval- and pear-shaped hand axes.

Approximately 100,000 years ago, Middle Paleolithic tool styles like the Aterian and Mousterian began appearing in the fossil record. The earliest known Aterian style tool, a rough spear or arrowhead, was discovered in Morocco dating back 145,000 years ago. The Middle Paleolithic also saw the invention of stone tipped spears. By 70,000 to 65,000 BP, smaller stone tools were also being created.

In the United States, Clovis points and, later, Folsom points, were used during the Paleolithic period by early hunters. Clovis points are often found with mammoth bones, while Folsom points are found mainly with bison.

Fire

It is believed that fire was used by Homo erectus and Homo ergaster as early as 300,000 to 1.5 million years ago. There is a possibility that its use dates even further back to hominin Homo habilis or even Australopithecines. However, the use of fire did not become common until the Middle Paleolithic or Middle Stone Age.

Neolithic

While the Stone Age saw the evolution of Homo erectus in the Lower Paleolithic, early Homo sapiens in the Middle Paleolithic, and the beginnings of modern human behavior in the Upper Paleolithic, the Neolithic is considered to be the "cradle of civilization."

It is also the final period of the Stone Age, dating from 10,000 to 4500 BCE. During this period there was a progression of cultural and behavioral changes that include the use of wild and domesticated crops, along with the domestication of animals.

The Neolithic began around 10,200 BCE in the Levant, the Mediterranean region of western Asia, by the Natufian culture. It is thought that their use of wild cereals is what evolved into early farming. This period overlaps with the Pre-Pottery Neolithic of 10,200–8800 BC. Along with their growing dependency on wild cereals, the return to glacial periods around 10,000 BC, otherwise known as the Younger Dryas, is thought to have contributed to the beginnings of a more sedentary way of life.

Farming communities had spread from Levant to Asia Minor, North Africa, and North Mesopotamia by 10,200–8800 BCE. Mesopotamia is also the site of the earliest Neolithic developments in 10,000 BCE. Early farming was limited to a small range of wild and domesticated plants. This included einkorn wheat, millet, and spelt. Sheep, goats, and dogs had also been domesticated by this time. Domesticated cattle and pigs are in evidence around 6900–6400 BCE. Permanent or seasonal settlements were also established, along with the use of pottery. The period before pottery in the Neolithic is PPNA.

It is important to note that not all societies developed culturally in the same order. For example, early Japanese and other East Asian cultures were using pottery before they started farming.

The Neolithic Pre-Pottery eras are divided into three stages, with two parts to the second one:

- Neolithic 1 (PPNA), of which the temple in Turkey, Göbekli Tepe, may be one of the first examples of, in roughly 10,000 BCE. The site was thought to have been built by early hunter-gatherer tribes and may be the earliest example of a "house of worship." The primary advancement during this time was the advent of farming and agriculture. There is also evidence of early grain and meat storage during this time.

- Neolithic 2 (PPNB), during which there are two periods, roughly beginning around 8800 BCE. During this period, rectangular mud-brick homes were built as single or multiple-room dwellings for families. Burial findings have suggested that an ancestor cult may have also developed during this period. This is when a society pays respect to their dead. Preserved skulls which have been plastered with mud to form facial features have been discovered. It is thought that once the body had decomposed, the skeleton was then buried underneath the floor or between buildings.

- Neolithic 2 (PPNC)—excavations at 'Ain Ghazal, Jordan have suggested that there was a later Pre-Pottery Neolithic C period. It is thought that it developed during the climatic crisis occurring in 6200 BCE, along with influences from cultures domesticating animals and hunter-gatherers from the southern Levant. These cultures eventually spread down the shoreline along the Red Sea into Syria and southern Iraq.

- Neolithic 3 (PN), which began around 6400 BCE in the Fertile Crescent. By this time, individual cultures had developed.

The Neolithic cultures were replaced during the Chalcolithic (Stone-Bronze Age) around 4500 BCE and the Bronze Age in approximately 3500 BCE.

Development of Civilization and Urban Societies

Throughout most of the Neolithic Period in Eurasia, people lived in small tribes composed of different family groups. Due to a lack of evidence, it's thought that social stratification did not truly develop until the Bronze Age. The earliest evidence of civilizations dates to 4000–3000 BCE in Mesopotamia and eventually Egypt. By 2500 BCE, civilizations were thriving in the Indus Valley. China saw its first civilizations around 1500 BCE and Central America in approximately 1200 BCE. By then, there were civilizations on every continent except Antarctica.

Due to farming, domestication of animals, and the changing climate, civilizations began developing around 6,000 years ago (4000 BCE). However, for archaeologists to refer to it as a civilization, it is necessary for it to have several characteristics. This includes:

1. large centers of population
2. unique art styles and monumental architecture
3. shared communication strategies/abilities—messenger runners, etc.
4. complex division of labor—building, farming, hunting, etc.
5. systems in place for administering territories
6. people divided into social and economic classes

Once these characteristics are present, it is considered a "civilization."

Urban areas developed from civilizations and can be found throughout the world. Teotihuacán in Mexico had a population as high as 200,000 residents from 300 to 600 BCE. The Khmer civilization is another example of an urban society which flourished in parts of Cambodia, Laos, Thailand, Vietnam, and Myanmar from 800 to 1400. The importance of urban areas is that it allows civilizations to develop, while also including rural regions in the population. Rural areas are necessary for farming, hunting, and fishing, which is necessary to feed urban populations. During this time, trade also began to develop between different civilizations. The rural populace also began trading their wares to urban dwellers.

CULTURAL SYSTEMS AND PROCESSES

Components of Culture

A society is considered a culture if five components are present: language, symbols, beliefs/values, norms, and artifacts. Anthropologists look for two basic components when classifying a society as a culture. These components are:

- nonmaterial, which refers to the language, symbols, and beliefs that define the society
- material, which refers to tools, technology, utensils, clothing, modes of transportation (walking, riding, boats, etc.), and any other physical artifacts

Symbols

Gestures, signs, signals, objects, and words are examples of symbols that are used to help understand experiences by conveying a specific message or meaning. A symbol can be a badge denoting an office or occupation. Jewelry like wedding bands and crowns are also example of symbols. They can be painted or carved onto artifacts or placed on a door or wall.

Symbols can also be gestures that let others know when to start moving or stand still. Some of the earliest examples of the use of symbols is thought to have been in Mesopotamia in the Early Bronze Age. The double-headed eagle seal was discovered on a scroll describing the foundation of Gudea, a city in southern Mesopotamia.

The earliest known forms of writing began with symbols by the ancient Sumerians around 3400–3100 BCE. Known as pre-cuneiform, it appeared along with Egyptian hieroglyphics on tablets, buildings, monuments, and scrolls around the same time. By 2600 BCE, the symbols were being arranged in coherent texts.

Language

Language, both written and spoken, is a symbol that is present in all cultures. A language is comprised of different symbols that, when put together, form an understandable work, not just a concept. Unlike symbols, language is constantly evolving as society changes.

For example, words used a generation ago "go out of style" and are replaced by newly created ones. Language can even vary by region, even if the people are part of the same culture. For example, the words "soda", "Coke", and "pop". Southerners are more likely to request a "COKE" even if they want a "Sprite", while Northerners are more apt to ask for a "soda" or the brand name of the desired drink.

Anthropologists theorize, from known evidence, that language first developed around 50,000–150,000 years ago. This coincides with the evolution of modern Homo sapiens. This "first" language is referred to as Proto-Human language.

Values and Beliefs

Values are what a culture uses to define what is "good or bad" behavior in the society. Values are an integral part of society and are crucial if teaching and transmitting a culture's beliefs. Just as important as values are a culture's beliefs. These are the convictions the society holds to be true. While specific beliefs are shared by most, if not all of the culture, collective values might apply to a lesser few. Specific beliefs and collective values are present in every culture. An example of one that can occur in the United States might be that the majority of Americans believe in the American dream—anyone willing to work hard enough will be wealthy and successful in life. The collective value is placed on the importance of wealth.

Values do give cultures guidelines on which behaviors are considered "good" or acceptable. However, values cannot enforce behavior. Values also change over generations or as collective societal beliefs evolve into new ones. Values also vary in different cultures. For example, in the United States, holding hands is a gesture/symbol of love. However, in some cultures it is only a sign of friendship and respect—in 2005, U.S. President George W. Bush was photographed holding hands with the Saudi Arabian Crown Prince. It was a gesture of goodwill, not romantic love.

Norms

Rules that are written and established are known as norms. While values can only provide guidance, norms can be enforced. Some examples of norms include laws, requirements for college entrance, employee manuals, along with traffic and other types of instructive signs. These are examples of formal norms that are strictly enforced and have known punishments.

There are also informal norms in a culture that are usually learned through observation, general socialization, and imitation. Some informal norms are also taught, such as holding the door for elders, and having proper table manners.

Norms can be further classified as mores (pronounced mor-ays) or folkways. Mores are the moral principles and views of a norm as a group. Some mores, like murder, are both immoral and illegal. Mores are not only enforced, but people that violate these norms are often disgraced and shunned. Folkways are norms without including moral principles. Instead, folkways dictate what is considered appropriate behaviors in common daily interactions, like whether or not to shake someone's hand or give a quick kiss on the cheek as a greeting.

Symbolic Systems

Symbolic systems in culture is the ability of the society to pass down learned behavioral traditions to other generations by the invention of systems that only exist symbolically. For example, a system of currency only exists as long as the culture believes in its value. Without belief, the system will fail.

Other examples of symbolic systems include lists of religious deities and belief in the underworld.

Followers of Darwin have found it difficult to explain the development of symbolic systems in cultures. One reason is that a symbolic system cannot be proven with scientific facts. This is one of the cornerstones of Darwin's theory for evolution, that man was not suddenly created, instead evolved over eons.

Previously it was believed that symbolic cultures emerged in Europe around 40,000 years ago during the transition from Middle to Upper Paleolithic. Recent discoveries suggest that it could date back farther to sub-Saharan Africa, during the Middle Stone Age, 100,000–200,000 years ago. These discoveries included ground ochre and geometric engravings on blocks of ochre that suggest it was possibly a cosmetics tool used for traditional rituals. Pierced shells were also found, suggesting a type of decoration.

Language and Communication

Language is defined as a set of arbitrary symbols that are the same for a group. The symbols that make up the language can be verbal, written, or signed. This is one of the main methods humans communicate. There are also nonverbal forms of communication that include body language and/or modification, along with hairstyle and clothing. Several non-human groups use a communication system. Primates, elephants, dolphins, and whales are just some examples. The difference is that this communication system is only comprised of calls. Each call has one specific meaning. For example, they can indicate a predator, food, water, etc.

Human Nonverbal Communication

Nonverbal communication is an extremely effective way to send and receive a simple message. Forms of nonverbal communication include body language, gestures, facial expressions, posture, and eye contact. Ray Birdwhistell (1918–1994) was the first to study nonverbal communication in humans. Today, it is studied with the use of technology.

Proxemics

The term proxemics was first used by anthropologist Edward T. Hall in 1966. It refers to the amount of space people need between themselves and someone else to feel comfortable. Proxemics is a sub-category of human nonverbal communication that is further divided into physical and personal territory. Proxemics does vary across cultures, often due to differences in population numbers.

Chronemics

This is the study of time and how it is used during nonverbal communication. A pause (nonverbal communication) during a conversation (verbal communication) can build anticipation without anything being said. Time can also play a role in terms of attention span and the reinforcement or expression of power in a relationship. How a culture perceives time influences everything from how they communicate to how they organize and execute daily activities.

Kinesics

The study of body movements and gestures is known as kinesics. This nonverbal form of communication can convey specific ideas, depending on how the movements are interpreted. This does vary across cultures. Ray Birdwhistell was the first anthropologist to use the term in 1952. He argued that every movement the body made meant something. He theorized that nothing was done by accident, and every movement expresses how the person is feeling.

 Posture

The position a person is holding their body is referred to as posture. It can also be a form of nonverbal communication. Mood and a person's level of self-esteem can often be determined from their posture. However, this is also one of the easiest forms of nonverbal communication to misunderstand.

 Gesture

Physical movements or gestures can range from full-body movements like dancing or hugging to smaller ones that only involve using the hands and arms. Facial features can also be gestures like a smile or a grimace. The meaning behind various gestures also differs from culture to culture.

 Eye Contact

One of the most important and expressive forms of nonverbal communication is eye contact. The signals vary from culture to culture and even religion. For example, in some cultures, not making eye contact is a sign of respect. In the United States, it is usually viewed as a sign of lying or guilt. However, too much eye contact can be seen as a sign of aggression.

 Sign Language

There are five types of sign language used around the world:
- American sign language,
- French sign language,
- Ethiopian sign language,
- Spanish sign language, and
- Arabic sign language.

Sign language is a formal language that uses a system of movements and hand gestures to communicate, instead of spoken words.

 Verbal Language

Human language differs from other forms of communication due to the linguistic rules it follows. Language is comprised of meaningful symbols that allow humans to communicate thoughts and ideas, some complex, with others. Language has several features that make it recognizable as human.

1. Duality of patterning, which is using the same symbols in varying order to create different sounds, like CAT/TACK/ACT.
2. Productivity, which is when rules and symbols can be combined for an infinite number of possible messages.
3. Interchangeability, in which speakers and listeners are both able to send and receive messages.
4. Arbitrariness, in which only sounds the word makes provide meaning; there are no other perceived associations. For example, the word "whale" only refers to the animal. It does not describe its size or the physicality of the subject or word.
5. Displacement in time and space, which allows for the use of past, present, and future tense.
6. Specialization, in which the only purpose of the language is for communication.
7. Cultural transmission, in which the specifics of the language must be learned and passed down through generations.

 Sapir-Whorf Hypothesis

In the 1900s, anthropologist Edward Sapir first theorized that language defines how a person thinks and behaves. He believed that language and thoughts are interwoven and that people are equally affected by the confines of their language. Following in his footsteps, Sapir's student, Benjamin Lee Whorf, theorized that language is not a way to voice ideas, it's what shapes the ideas before they're spoken. Known as linguistic determinism, it states that a person cannot think outside the confines of their language.

 Cultural Diffusion and Power

Cultural diffusion was first theorized by Leo Frobenius, a German ethnologist and archaeologist, in 1898. It was defined as the spread of cultural ideas, religions, styles, technologies, and languages. It can occur between individuals from a single culture or from one culture to another. Some of the better-known examples of cultural diffusion are the spread of the chariot for war and iron smelting in ancient times, and automobiles and western-style suits in the twentieth century.

Since its conception, five major types of cultural diffusion have been defined as

1. expansion diffusion, an idea or innovation that develops and stays within a cultural while also spreading out to others
2. relocation diffusion, the idea or innovation that moves with the culture to a new location while leaving traces of its origin behind
3. hierarchical diffusion, the innovation or idea is spread from larger places to smaller ones, often ignoring distances and usually influenced by the socially elite
4. contagious diffusion, in which the idea or innovation spreads from person to person within a specific culture
5. stimulus diffusion, an idea or innovation that is spread with another concept

Intercultural diffusion can occur when populations migrate, taking their culture with them. Trans-cultural visitors, merchants, sailors, slaves, diplomats, soldiers, and hired artisans can bring ideas and innovations with them. Marriages between cultures can also trade ideas, as well as through the trade of letters and books. In modern times, technology can help spread ideas across cultural boundaries.

There are several theories that are used to explain intercultural diffusion that include

- Migrationism, where cultural ideas are spread by gradual or sudden population movements.
- Culture circles, which is the theory that larger cultures originated from smaller ones.
- The term "cultural bullet," penned by J.P. Mallory is a model that looks at invasion versus gradual migration versus diffusion. This theory suggests that the continuation of the material culture and social organization are more important and stronger than the continuation of the culture's language. In other words, a society's language is more likely to change than their material cultural or how they're organized socially.
- Hyperdiffusionism, which theorizes that all cultures originated from a single one.

Cultural power is often referred to as cultural diplomacy. Its goal is to foster the ex change of ideas and views, along with building bridges between different cultures. The peaceful exchange of ideas and innovations can help various cultures evolve and thrive in a world that is constantly changing.

Cultural Universals

Cultural universals are elements, patterns, traits, or institutions that are common globally, yet still differ such as with modes of behavior and values. Some examples of cultural universals include:

- gender roles
- taboo on incest
- religious and healing rituals
- marriage
- mythology
- art
- dance
- music
- games
- cooking

Some anthropologists deny or reduce the importance of cultural universals, theorizing that these traits were inherited biologically and are the result of nature, not nurture. These anthropologists refer to the previous examples as "empty universals." However, there is evidence dating back to the Upper Paleolithic indicating the emergence of behavioral modernity. Some of the anthropologists and sociologists that first began studying the importance of cultural universals include George Murdock, Claude Lévi-Strauss, and Donald Brown.

Sub-Cultures

A sub-culture is a smaller group within a larger one. Ethnic sub-cultures share the customs, language, and food of their heritage, while existing within a larger and different culture. Sub-cultures can also unite due to shared experiences. This can apply to motorcycle clubs or even members of an addiction or other type of self-help group.

Counter-Cultures

Counter-cultures are separated from sub-cultures primarily by behavior by sociologists. While sub-cultures typically still have the same beliefs and values of the larger group, the same is often not true for counter-cultures. Members of counter-cultures often eschew the values, behaviors, and norms of the larger society. Instead, they create their own and in some cases even exist only on the primary culture's edges.

World Systems

The world systems theory seeks to explain the reasons for the rise and fall of nations, imperialism, social unrest, and income inequality. It is a multidisciplinary approach to work history and social change.

The best-known version of world systems analysis was developed by Immanuel Wallerstein in the early 1970s. He began by tracing the start of a capitalist world economy from the 1450s to 1640. Wallerstein believed that capitalism was the outcome of a protracted feudalism crisis (1290–1450). It was during this time that Europe used its advantages and took control over the majority of the world's economy, and presided over the development and spread of industrialism, and a capitalist economy. This indirectly resulted in unequal development.

World system theories date to the 1970s and were created to replace the modernization theory. Wallerstein criticized the later theory for three reasons:

1. Its only unit of analysis was the nation state.
2. It assumed that there is only one path for evolutionary development and it applies to all countries.
3. It doesn't account for transnational structures that slow or block local and national development.

There were three previous theories that influenced Wallerstein's world system theory. One was the Annales school, which focuses on using long term processes and geo-ecological regions as the unit of analysis. The second was Marxism, which focuses on the stress of social conflict, especially among classes. The final was the dependency theory, which is an explanation of the development processes.

The main difference between Wallerstein's theory and the dependency theory is that Wallerstein did not believe that a core country (one in control) would willingly exploit a poorer country.

Colonialism

The act and practice of extending control over weaker areas or people is the definition of colonialism. There are four types:

1. settler colonialism, which is large-scale migration
2. exploitation colonialism, which focuses on exploiting natural resources
3. surrogate colonialism, in which a settlement is supported by the colonial power
4. internal colonialism, which is the idea that there is an uneven structural power between areas of the state or government

Colonialism can be traced back to the Phoenicians, Egyptians, Greeks, and Romans. All of these cultures flourished and expanded. The first three cultures were from 1500 BCE to 300 BCE, followed by the Romans. In the seventh century, Arab cultures colonized large portions of the Middle East and Northern Africa, along with parts of Europe and Asia. By the ninth century, the Venetians, Genovese, and Amalfians began expanding until the Fourth Crusade in 1204 with the declaration of the acquisition of three octaves of the Byzantine Empire. This marked the start of the Latin Empire.

Modern colonialism began with Prince Henry the Navigator, a Portuguese explorer in the fifteenth century that started the Age of Exploration. In the seventeenth century, the French and Dutch colonial empires were established following the Portuguese and Spanish. The British Empire was also established in the seventeenth century, along with a Danish colonial empire and a Swedish one. The end of WWI saw many of the old colonial empires fall, along with the end of WWII.

Arts

The study of art in anthropology is considered a sub-field of social anthropology. It focuses on the historical, aesthetic, and economical aspects of non-Western art forms. This includes the study of what is referred to as "tribal art."

Two anthropologists that studied art in its many forms were Franz Boas (often considered the father of modern anthropology) in his 1927 book Primitive Arts in which he provides a detailed case study of "primitive" art forms, primarily along the Pacific Northwest coast, and Claude Levi-Strauss, who took Boas' analysis further in his published book The Way of the Masks. In it, he traced changes in the plastic form of the masks from Northwest Pacific indigenous peoples. He theorized that the masks showed patterns of intercultural interaction between the various indigenous peoples along the coast.

Anthropologists study art differently than other social scientists. Using ethnographic methods as a primary form of research, anthropologists focus on "holism." This is the paradigm that theorizes the life of an individual must be understood through the study of a person's complete life. This means their situation and activity. Anthropologists believe that the study of art goes beyond aesthetics. Art is a complex set of relationships that contribute to the creation of a society.

 Brief History of Notable Art Discoveries

The first examples of Stone Age art were created during the Lower Paleolithic (300,000–1,000,000 BCE). Descendants of Homo erectus, the first early humans to migrate from Africa, are believed to have been the first to draw images on or pound holes into rocks. From approximately 100,000 to 40,000 BCE the first prehistoric sculptors and cave paintings of anatomically correct humans emerged (Homo neanderthalensis).

While the cultural and aesthetic significance of the first prehistoric artworks is not known by anthropologists, they are convinced that some of the discovered forms of art took a monumental effort by several people. For example, cupules—a term first used by archeologist Robert G. Bednarik to describe the small holes pounded into rocks, often walls, during the Stone Age.

Sculptures of human figures have been discovered dating back to around 38,000 BCE. The first discovered was a semi-male sculpture found in the Hohlenstein-Stadel cave in Swabian Jura, Germany. The oldest recorded sculpture of a woman dates to around 30,000 BCE during the Upper Paleolithic.

Ceramic art can be dated back to 26,000 BCE, known as the Venus of Dolní Věstonice. During the late Paleolithic, ceramic pottery was being used in China's Jiangxi province. The piece of ancient pottery dates to approximately 18,000 BCE.

Megalithic architecture was erected during the Neolithic Period of the Stone Age, and throughout the Chalcolithic and Bronze Ages. Some megalithic monuments have been approximately dated to 8000 BCE.

Bronze Age art did not develop at the same time throughout the world. Some cultures, like China's, that were more advanced and lacked the materials, skipped to the Iron Age and then went back to develop bronze artifacts. As of now, the oldest known prehistoric bronze sculpture was produced by the Maikop culture around 3500 BCE in the Russian North Caucasus region.

Other forms of artwork that followed these early examples include metalwork in Mesopotamia.

Marriage and Family Patterns

Family and marriage is a social invention and a cultural construct. This means that it was created and not formed by nature/evolution. While primates and some other species of mammals do "recognize" family groups, and some animals (swans and wolves to name a few) do mate for life, only humans prefer marriage ceremonies.

Even though families exist in all global societies, there are variations across cultures. Some of these variations include:

- how people relate to each other
- how marriage partners are found
- when people should have children
- who cares for the children
- how property is passed down

The first known recorded evidence of a marriage ceremony that joined a man and woman together as a life couple dates to approximately 2350 BCE in Mesopotamia. The marriage ceremony evolved over several hundred years, being embraced by the ancient Hebrews, Egyptians, Greeks, Romans, and other cultures.

It wasn't until the end of the eighteenth century and into the nineteenth that enlightened thinkers first put forth the idea that marriage should be about love. These early thinkers stated that they were promoting "the right to personal happiness." Until the first recorded marriage ceremony, a majority of these unions between a man and a woman were treated as "business arrangements." Typically, one or both families stood to gain land, animals, money, and/or prominence through a marriage.

Lewis Henry Morgan, a lawyer and anthropologist that studied Native American cultures, documented words used by the Iroquois to depict various family members. He stated that these words were important since the terms indicated certain responsibilities and rights the individual had within the family and society. This is similar to the labels Westerners place on family members, e.g., aunt or father.

The concept of status and role expected by individuals in the family was first used by Ralph Linton, a mid-twentieth century anthropologist that published *The Study of Man* and *The Tree of Culture*. Both works discuss how status and role are defined in families across cultures.

- Status is defined as a culturally-designated position an individual holds in the family, like a mother, father, aunt, sister, cousin, grandmother, etc.
- Role is defined as a set of behaviors that are expected of that individual and others that hold the same status in their families.

Roles, like status, are cultural ideals and can differ widely across cultures and even generations. For example, during the early twentieth century, a mother's role was to care for the home and children. Today, a mother's role often includes earning a working wage. The role for fathers has also changed, with many more staying home to care for the house and children.

Origin of Family Through World Cultures

In the majority of world cultures, families began with a creation myth. The ancient Hebrews followed the story written down in Genesis, while the ancient Greek poet Hesiod described the destruction of the four previous Ages of Men that finally culminated in the creation of modern humans.

The ancient Hebrews believed in a patriarchal world, and the practice of polygamy is mentioned throughout biblical times. Polygamy is the practice of one man taking more than a single wife. This was a common practice throughout the ancient world, particularly in what is now the Middle East and parts of Asia. Men in biblical times also started recording their descent (when applicable) from the prophet Moses in order to be accepted into the early Jewish priesthood.

Roman families were also patriarchal, where the father was the leader and authoritarian in the family. Known as pater familias, Roman family leaders listed everyone in the household, including grown children and slaves. While it was not uncommon for family fathers to have children outside of the marriage, these offspring were not allowed to inherit their father's name or belongings. Instead, these children belong to the family and society groups of their mothers. These relationships outside of marriage were "concubinage" and were common and legal throughout the Roman Empire.

Cultures throughout Assyria, China, and Egypt all kept detailed records of the successors to ruling dynasties. Not only did this legitimize their power to rule as given to them by a "divine being," but it also reduced conflict when it was time to succeed the previous ruler. There are some similarities between various cultures and succession. Both the Incas (king) and Egyptians (pharaoh) believed their right to rule came from the Sun God. Lines of succession were not always written down when the records first started. Instead, cultures such as the Kinte of Africa, Inca of South America, and the Maori of New Zealand passed the family records down orally.

Symbols were also used to record lineage. For example, the totem poles commonly found along the American Pacific Northwest—the totem pole is a symbolic representation of their ancestors' history and family identity. The poles are also seen as being tied to the spirit world.

In the Middle Ages (fifth to fifteenth centuries), European nobility had long, well-documented family histories. In 1538, England's King Henry VIII mandated that churches begin keeping records, and the practice spread throughout Europe. One of the earliest known genealogy records from Europe dates to 1086, known as the Doomsday Book, and covers much of England and Wales.

 Kinship and Descent Groups

Kinship is the term used to describe culturally recognized family ties. Kinship includes both consanguineal (blood ties) and affinal (ties through marriage). Kinship can also be chosen or created. For example, adoption is culturally recognized as a legitimate form of kinship.

There is a lot of variation cross-culturally in families. However, anthropologists have organized a broad kinship system. This refers to the culturally recognized relationships between members of the same family. How the kinship system is created does vary by culture.

- Patrilineal descent follows the paternal family line from father to offspring.
- Matrilineal descent follows the maternal family line from mother to offspring.

Both of these kinship systems are considered unilineal since it only follows the descent from one side of the family. For some cultures, matrilineal descent is viewed as more authentic for the simple fact it can be proven that a mother gave birth, while it is more difficult to show (without DNA) if the man is the father.

The type of descent also determines if the family's last name will follow the father or mother. In the United States, traditionally, women take on the man's last name after marriage. However, this is changing throughout the Western world. It is no longer uncommon for women to keep their birth given last names or hyphenate it with their husbands. Some men also choose to take the family last name of their wives.

Along with unilinear descent, there is also bilateral descent. Bilateral refers to families that are defined by the descent from both the father and the mother. This is becoming more common, especially with the growing interest in ancestry and family history.

 ## Family Structures

Anthropologists describe family structures as a typical or preferred unit in a culture. There are several classification of family types that reflect the values and beliefs of the culture:

1. Nuclear families have parents in a culturally recognized relationship (often marriage) with dependent children. This is also referred to as a conjugal family. A non-conjugal nuclear family would be known today as a single-parent household.
2. Extended families are when at least three generations of one family sharing a household. Typically, this would be grandparents, parents, and children.
3. Stem families are a version of an extended family, where only one or more adult children live in the home with their spouse and children.

The family structure also influences rules of inheritance. In most cultures, it is the oldest living son. However, in Burma and Myanmar, it is the youngest daughter that is named as a beneficiary. This is because the older children are expected to marry and support their families, while the youngest daughter is in the best position to carry on for the aging parents.

In many Western cultures, the rules of inheritance have changed to typically include all offspring as beneficiaries. While this has changed in Western cultures, once a marriage occurs in patrilinear societies, the wife takes the husband's residence and vice versa in matrilineal societies.

Three other types of family structures are:
- The joint family is a large multigenerational family. Both married and unmarried family members, siblings reside in the same household. One example of a large extended family can be found in Croatia, where dozens of family members live together.
- Polygamous families are based on a man having multiple wives or, in rare cases, a wife having multiple husbands. While multiple wives were common in some ancient cultures, in the Western world it is discouraged, if not illegal. Polygyny is one husband with multiple wives. Polyandry is one wife with multiple husbands.

- Step families are blended families where children from their parents' previous relationships are brought together. The siblings are not related by blood, but due to their respective parent's marriage, they are now considered to be step-brothers/sisters.

 ## Culture and Marriage

Many cultures have rules stating who a person can marry within their society. These rules are known as endogamy. If the cultural expectations allow for marriage outside of the group, it is referred to as exogamy. These rules can also prohibit marriages between close family members, e.g., brothers and sisters, or even first cousins.

While it is frowned upon and in some cases illegal to marry close family members in the Western world, as close as the eighteenth century, some European aristocrats and royals were engaged to and married first cousins. This was done primarily to keep any wealth in the family.

There are some Middle Eastern cultures where patrilateral cousin marriage is still preferred. This is when someone marries a male or female cousin on their father's side. Other cultures prefer that marriages between cousins take place from the mother's side, e.g., her brothers or sisters. These are referred to as cross-cousins.

Arranged marriages are still popular in many cultures around the world, even in the United States. A marriage can be arranged through family members, friends, a community matchmaker, and now even via dating websites.

 ## Social and Economic Stratification

Social stratification refers to how society categorizes its people into groups based on certain socioeconomic factors that include:

- wealth
- income
- race
- education
- gender
- occupation
- social status

In Western cultures, social stratification is generally categorized into three classes:

1. upper class
2. middle class
3. lower class

These three categories can be further divided into upper middle class, etc. The social stratification in a society can also be based on kinship, clan, tribe, caste, or all four.

There are four underlying principles in social stratification. These are

1. Social stratification as a product of society and not the individual.
2. Social stratification as passed down/reproduced from generation to generation. For example, this would be like passing down inherited titles or wealth.
3. Social stratification as present in all cultures, though it can vary.
4. Social stratification involving inequality, along with beliefs and attitudes about social status.

When describing social stratification, economics/income is the most common variable used. However, it can limit how anthropologists view the family and culture as a whole. There are two types of stratification systems: closed and open. Closed systems allow for very little change in social position, and often prohibit socializing between classes. Open systems are based on achievement, not birth or marriage. An open system allows for movement and interaction between the classes.

An example of a closed system is the caste system. It is one where people will have the same status they were born into throughout their lives. A class system is open. People do not have to remain in the same social class they were born into.

BANDS, TRIBES, CHIEFDOMS & STATES

American cultural anthropologist Elman Service (1915–1996) created what is now known as sociopolitical typology. It refers to four types/levels of a political organization:

1. hunter-gatherers (foragers)/bands
2. horticulture/tribes
3. pastoralism/chiefdoms
4. agriculture/states

Ethnographic and archaeological studies across the globe have shown several correlations between economic, social, and political organizations.

Bands

Previously referred to as "camps" or "hordes," bands were the simplest form of society. They typically consisted of a small kin group, no larger than an extended family/clan. Modern anthropologists generally agree that a band contained between thirty to fifty clan/family members.

Bands were usually loosely organized, and some even split up into summer or winter camps. Non-primary family members could also leave to join other bands. The power structure was primarily egalitarian. This means that the best hunter-gatherers were recognized, but this did not give them authority over other clan members. Any judgments against a clan member would be decided by the band's elders. This type of governing body by a band's elders eventually evolved into the more complex societies that arose with the start of sedentary agriculture.

A. R. Radcliffe-Brown, an English social anthropologist, defined a band as a fundamental unit of Australian social organizations according to these five criteria:

1. It describes people that normally share the same camp and lifestyle.
2. It is the primary landowner of the territory.
3. Each band is independent and autonomous. Social life is regulated by a camp council generally comprised of the band's elders.
4. Children are permitted to join the father's band, even out of wedlock.
5. A unified band/clan identity is established with all external groups.

Some historical examples of band societies include the Shoshone of the Great Basin in the U.S., the Bushmen of Southern Africa, and the pygmies (Mbuti) of the Ituri Forest in Africa. This also includes several bands of indigenous Australians.

Tribes

Horticulture is the agriculture of plants, primarily for food, materials, beauty, comfort, and decoration. American horticulturist Liberty Hyde Bailey describes it as "…the growing of flowers, fruits and vegetables, and of plants for ornament and fancy."

As a study, horticulture has a long history that can be dated back to Cyrus the Great (600–530 BCE and founder of the Achaemenid Empire/First Persian Empire). However, the practice of horticulture is even older. Taro and yam cultivation in Papua New Guinea has been dated to at least 6950–6440 BCE. It is believe by anthropologists that the beginnings of horticulture occurred in the transition from bands to tribes.

Hunter-gatherer bands began cultivating various crops in small plots around their dwellings, or larger ones that were only used during migration from one camp to another. One example is the milpa (maize fields) in Mesoamerican cultures. Pre-Columbian rainforest tribes are believed to have been among the first to enhance soil productivity by using smoldering plant waste or biochar. In modern terms, this practice is known as "slash and burn." The left-over plants from the harvest are burned to fertilize the soil that is left fallow for at least one growing season. This prevents all the nutrients plants need to flourish from being drained from the soil by previous harvests.

There are two ways that horticulture differs from agriculture. First, it is done on a smaller scale, often with various plants mixed together. Secondly, it includes a wide variety of crops, including fruit trees. Agriculture typically focuses on one type of plant/crop.

The first plants early hunter-gatherers and tribes are thought to have grown are:

1. emmer wheat
2. einkorn wheat
3. hulled barley
4. peas
5. lentils
6. bitter vetch
7. chick peas
8. flax

These eight crops were thought to be first domesticated around 9500 BCE. However, wild grains were eaten, collected for seeds, and grown at least by 105,000 BCE. China was growing domesticated rice by 6200 BCE. Tribes also began domesticating animals. The first were pigs in Mesopotamia around 11,000 BCE, followed by sheep around 11,000–9000 BCE. Cattle were first domesticated from wild aurochs in what is now known as modern Turkey and Pakistan around 8500 BCE.

Tribes are similar to bands in that they are comprised primarily of family and clan members. Different lineages can exist simultaneously in a tribe. A tribe is based on several criteria:

- kinship/clan
- ethnicity ("race")
- language

- dwelling place
- religious beliefs
- oral traditions/cultural practices
- political group

Tribes are considered to be a political unit formed from an organization of family or families. Tribal structures are thought to have been flexible in order to adapt to changing situations. This allowed them to coordinate production and the distribution of food when there was a scarcity by preventing members from stockpiling during times when there was plenty.

Chiefdoms

A chiefdom is a type of hierarchical political organization in a society that is not industrial. It is typically based on kinship and the leadership position is held by senior members of select families or houses.

Elman Service noted that chiefdoms, within the bounds of cultural evolution, are more complex than bands and tribes, but not as complex as states or civilizations. The political leader of a chiefdom is the chief.

There are at least two social classes present in a chiefdom: elite and commoner, though ancient Hawaiian chiefdoms have held up to four social classes. In a chiefdom, a single lineage or family line holds power that is transferred down to the next generation. Typically, this would be the father to the eldest son.

A single chiefdom is usually a central community that is near or surrounded by smaller ones. All of the communities may have different family lineages, but all answer to the chief with the centralized hereditary power. Each of the smaller communities can have their own leaders that still answer to the chief.

Chiefdoms can also be more complex. Several chiefdoms can exist under the power of a larger one. However, anthropologists have noted in their research that single/simple and complex chiefdoms were often unstable. Tribal units would band together to form a chiefdom, only to break apart due to strife or stress and possibly reform again. One example of this type of disorganization was the Germanic tribes that eventually conquered the western Roman Empire in the fifth century.

States

The undisputed definition of a state is "a polity under a system of governance." There are different types of states, as classified by political philosophers:

- sovereign, in which the state is not dependent on or under another state or power
- hegemony, in which the ultimate sovereignty is in another state
- federal, in which it is part of a federal union of other states

A state can be separate from a government. The state is an organization while a government is comprised of a specific group of people. States can also differ from nations. A state can be made up of a single ethnicity, while a nation can be multi-ethnic.

The earliest examples of a state emerged with writing and agriculture. With agriculture, a new social class emerged that no longer was needed as hunter-gatherers. The free time allowed this small group to develop writing, which made it possible to have information in a centralized location.

Even though states existed in some form before the ancient Greek empire, the Greeks are thought to be the first to have a political philosophy and political institutions. However, the ancient Sumerians are believed to be the first culture to use "zero" in calculations. During the fifth to ninth centuries, states were organized according to the principles of feudalism. Feudalism is the exchange of services for the privilege of working the land. Those that worked the land were referred to as serfs or peasants. From feudalism, other social hierarchies evolved.

City-states also existed in Mesoamerica. While the Olmecs were the first major Mesoamerican culture from around 1400 BCE and thrived for around one thousand years, they did not build any major cities that are known. However, one pyramid attributed to the Olmecs has been discovered, along with nine-foot-high stone heads that resemble African warriors. The Olmecs did have writing (hieroglyphics) and were primarily farmers, artists, astronomers, and mathematicians.

The Maya, however, are thought to be the first Mesoamerican civilization, beginning around 2600 BCE. While, as a people, the Maya are the eldest, they did not emerge as a city-state until 250–900 AD, when the majority of their cities were built. One of the largest cities built by the Maya is Chichen Itza on the Yucatan Peninsula. It was one of the major seats of power for the Maya from around 600 to 1221 AD.

Farther away, in modern day Peru, the Incas created their own city-states. Their vast civilization extended over 2,500 miles and at its height had a population of sixteen million. The Inca had laws, an army, irrigation, bridges, roads, and tunnels. What they did not have was writing. The Incans thrived from around 1200 AD to 1533, when it fell to Spanish invaders.

The youngest city-state in Mesoamerica was the Aztecs. They built their city-states from around 1325 AD, starting with Tenochtitlan. The Aztecs conquered most of the area around the city, falling to the Spanish in 1521.

These early states created the conditions that led to the emergence of modern European states, now referred to as countries.

 Subsistence and Settlement Patterns

Since the start of anthropology in the mid-1800s, researchers have been trying to classify the various world cultures. By classifying cultures, anthropologists believe a wide range of behavioral patterns could be explained.

In the nineteenth and into the early twentieth century, there were only two types of classification—primitive and civilized. During the late nineteenth century, anthropologists like Edward B. Tylor (England) and Lewis Henry Morgan (U.S.) made slight refinements to the previous classification system—savages, barbarians, and civilized peoples. The classification of cultures changed once more in the 1930s due to a large amount of ethnographic data. Anthropologists used differences in subsistence patterns to base their classifications. These classifications are still in use today. They are:

1. foraging, like hunter-gatherers
2. pastoralism, through herding large domesticated animals
3. horticulture, in small-scale farming
4. intensive agriculture through large-scale farming

Foraging is the oldest subsistence pattern. Human societies all relied on it until around 10,000 years ago. Foraging societies obtained most, if not all, their resources directly from the environment. Since they did not cultivate any of their resources, these early bands of people were almost continuously on the move. They did not erect any permanent structures, only temporary shelters if none were available in their surroundings (e.g., caves).

Pastoralism refers to the herding and breeding of domesticated animals. It is common in arid regions where inconsistent rainfall discourages farming as a lifestyle. Since the domesticated herds need to graze, pastoral communities are largely nomadic. It is still popular in Africa and Asia, with over twenty-one million pastoralists. Due to their nomadic nature, pastoralists rarely erect permanent structures, though it is believed that some early societies did build the occasional monolithic temple.

Horticulture is small-scale farming and allows for a population expansion. Anthropologists believe that the start of early settlements was a direct result of horticulture. A steady supply of food was always available, allowing the population to settle in one place.

Intensive agriculture differs from horticulture in that it requires the use of large parcels of land. It involves complex technology, even in ancient times, that includes planting, irrigating, plowing, fertilizing, and harvesting. Agriculture can also include raising livestock. Agrarian societies were generally larger than other ones and the increased population, combined with a reliable food source, allowed for the eventual rise of city-states.

By classifying the different cultures into those four groups, anthropologists are able to see how the first settlements arose that eventually gave way to city-states, and finally present-day cultures.

TRADE, RECIPROCITY, REDISTRIBUTION

A brief explanation of trade, reciprocity, redistribution, and market exchange is

- Trade is the exchange of goods/services for something a person or society needs (e.g., spices for silk).
- Reciprocity is the exchange of goods for something of equal value (like gift-giving).
- Redistribution redirects the goods to a central authority that then delivers it to the populace.
- Market exchange is commerce through a price on goods in a market.

Trade

The main facility of prehistoric peoples was trade. The history of long-distance commerce can be traced back to approximately 150,000 years ago. Between 35,000 and 30,000 BCE, trade among Homo sapiens developed in the Mediterranean. During the Stone Age, peoples traded flint and obsidian. However, trade is thought by anthropologists to have initially started in Southwest Asia.

Trade not only involved the exchange of goods and services, but ideas and knowledge as well. Trade was the major form of exchange before currency.

Reciprocity

Anthropologist Marshall Sahlins observed, in 1965, that there were three types of reciprocity that can be found in cultures around the globe:

1. Generalized reciprocity is gift-giving without expecting one in return.
2. Balanced reciprocity occurs when a gift is given and one is expected in return.
3. Negative reciprocity occurs when someone tries to make another give up something they want to keep. It can also be when a person tries to give a less expensive gift than the one they received.

Reciprocity in all forms is common in almost every culture. In some, it is the chief/leader that gives gifts to the populace, while in others, it is done to show love, friendship, and/or respect. It can also occur between leaders of different cultures as a greeting. What reciprocity does not do is increase the wealth of the society as a whole.

Redistribution

Redistribution of goods occurs in cultures around the world. Also referred to as redistribution exchanges, it is a system that allows for the even distribution of wealth throughout the society. For example, food items go to a centralized location and is then passed out to the populace. In modern Western cultures, examples of redistribution exchanges are charities and progressive tax brackets that are based on an individual's income.

One of the most elaborate redistribution exchanges is the potlatch, a ceremony practiced by indigenous peoples of the American Northwest Coast. The chief throws a large feast and distributes his wealth among the people. There is no wealth lost since it remains in their society. These gifts are often reciprocated at later events, when wealth is returned to the chief by the people.

Market Exchange

Market exchanges need institutions to govern them. This is because, in a market exchange, prices are set. This also includes an exchange of goods. Markets do not have to be stationary, but they are regulated by supply and demand.

Since markets are based on transactions, wealth is not evenly distributed among the populace. For example, if an individual is unable to feed their family in a reciprocal society, the group as a whole would share their wealth. In a market exchange, if a person cannot afford the item, they will have to go without. Wealth is not evenly distributed; it is only available to those that can afford it.

Modern Political Systems

The study of modern political systems (political anthropology) began in the nineteenth century when anthropologists started trying to trace the evolution of human societies. Due to the limited terms used to classify various cultures (e.g., primitive or savage), the early results were often speculative and even "racist."

Modern studies were built off of the early ones, particularly by Charles Darwin. He and other like-minded anthropologists focused on kinship to understand political organizations. For example, the role of lineage or genealogy was emphasized as part of these studies.

Contemporary political anthropology began with the publication of African Political Systems in 1940, edited by Meyer Fortes and E. E. Evans-Pritchard. They disagreed with the speculative theories put forth by earlier researchers, stating that "a scientific study of political institutions must be inductive and comparative and aim solely at establishing and explaining the uniformities found among them and their interdependencies with other features of social organization" (p.4). Their goal was to use taxonomy to classify societies into smaller categories, and then compare them to make generalizations about them. From there, political anthropology continued to evolve until now, where the study includes research on how European colonialism affects various political systems, along with the evolution of a culture's social systems.

In the 1980s, studies of modern political systems replaced "kinship" with "identity" and "identity politics." This also included a rise in nationalism, which is partially a state-produced culture. From there it has progressed to studies conducted in companies and bureaucratic structures. Modern political anthropology has become increasingly political, with current groups in power requesting their own specific studies in an effort to prove or change policy that affects the culture as a whole.

Globalization and the Environment

Dr. Alan Grainger, Senior Lecturer in Global Change and Policy at the University of Leeds, stated that it can be understood as "an increasing spatial uniformity and contentedness in regular environmental management practices." Citing an earlier work by William Clark, Dr. Grainger distinguished three aspects of environmental globalization:

- global flows of energy, materials, and organisms
- forming and obtaining worldwide acceptance of ideas about the global environment
- environmental governance, an ever-growing web of institutions concerned with the world's environment

Dr. Grainger has also noted that globalization and the environment are not new, and in fact can be found in the colonial era. The colonial era is roughly during the late Middle Age (1500s) to the start of the Age of Revolutions (1800s). During this period, Dr. Grainger states that the precursors to modern environmental globalization were researching how to create forests and restore old ones that were disappearing as the need for wood/lumber grew.

Environmental globalization is relatively new, only gaining momentum and acceptance in the last half of the twentieth century. This is unlike globalization of economic, cultural, and political norms which were already being pursued as popular fields of study in the nineteenth century.

Supporters of environmental globalization are generally non-government organizations and governments of developed countries. Governments of under-developed countries are often opposed to environmental globalization, believing that it is economically restrictive. The World Trade Organization (WTO) also supports free trade over environmental globalization.

Belief Systems

Without a belief system, religion would not exist. Beliefs cannot be proven true by science, although it is still thought to be true by followers of the religion. A belief system can include the mythological, supernatural, and/or spiritual aspects of the religion. Beliefs are different than religious practices. Some believers do not attend/observe religious practices but still consider themselves to be "of the faith." However, even though religion can be practiced by non-believers, it will not last through following generations.

Religious beliefs are derived from ideas that are exclusive to that religion. These beliefs often deal with the existence, characteristics, and worship of a deity or deities. The idea of divine intervention in the universe and in human life is a constant in most religions. Religious beliefs also serve to explain the "unexplainable" in the universe and life. A religious or spiritual leader passes the teaching down. Religious beliefs are also usually codified. For example, the Ten Commandments found in the Judean-Christian bible.

Fundamentalism

The term "fundamentalism" was first used to describe anti-modern Protestants in the U.S. In religious connotation, it is strict adherence to the scriptures as they were interpreted by conservative theologians. In the media, religious fundamentalists are portrayed as zealots and fanatics. There is no room for new interpretations of scripture in a fundamentalist religion. It does not evolve as times change.

Orthodoxy

Orthodoxy was first used to describe early Christians, and now the term denotes religious beliefs that closely follow the original edicts, hermeneutics, and apologies of the religious authority. In Christianity, it was the first communion of bishops (Magisterium). Orthodox Christianity can be found across the globe, with large communities in Greece, Russia, and Eastern Europe.

Modernism/Reform

During the Renaissance and the Enlightenment in Europe, different degrees of religious tolerance grew. Tolerance toward old and new religious ideas became more common. Philosophies were developed that challenged some of the more fantastical claims of religion, along with religious authority. Liberalizing political and social movements also moved religious reform along. Two examples are Reform Judaism and Liberal Christianity, where rationality, individual liberty, and equality have been integrated into their religious belief system.

Anthropologists and sociologists look for reasons why religious beliefs are important and society adheres to them. Some of the reasons theorized are:

- Belief in a deity is necessary for setting the rules for moral behavior.
- Religious practices can be serene and conducive to religious experiences, which enforces the beliefs.
- A sense of community is often felt with organized religion. Since everyone has the small beliefs, values, and morals, it can make people feel accepted and in a place they belong.
- By following religious practices and beliefs, a worshipper can feel closer to the divine.

James Alcock, a Canadian educator, also added that prayer and religious belief can help ease fear and anxiety, both of which are still common feelings in today's society.

Mythology

The term myth can mean different things:

1. A familiar story that retells historical events in a context to explain a belief, practice, or natural phenomenon. One of the most known collection of myths in the Western world comes from ancient Greece.
2. A person or thing that has an unverified existence or is imaginary.
3. A metaphor for the spiritual potentiality in a human.

Formal Institutions

Typically, only organized religions can have formal institutions. These institutions include schools at all grade levels. Religious homes for the disadvantaged or aging clergy and other church members, along with children's homes, can all be considered institutions if it is supported by that religion. However, a formal institution can also be the religion.

Organized religions seem to have grown in prevalence during the Neolithic era, when agriculture gave rise to wide-scale civilization. Many of these organized religions are still in existence today and include:

- Christianity

- Islam
- Judaism
- Sikhism
- Buddhism
- Hinduism

There are also loosely organized religions that include prehistoric, Native American, and other indigenous religions. There are also folk religions that include traditional African religions. These religions differ from traditional or organized religions but still have a strong belief system.

Cargo cults are another loosely organized religion, practiced by an "under-developed" society. This belief system practices superstitious rituals where the spirits are asked to bring modern goods, typically from a more technologically-advanced society. One example of a cargo cult can be found in the Melanesian Islands.

When religion first started is under debate, though the oldest known religion still in practice is Hinduism, dating back 4000 to 5000 years. The first known human burial occurred in 100,000 BCE in the Middle East. The earliest known cremated, anatomically-correct human dates back to around 40,000 BCE near Lake Mungo in New South Wales, Australia. While burials continued throughout prehistory, the first erected monument to religion (possibly a temple) is Göbekli Tepe in Turkey, dating back to around 9130–7370 BCE.

Throughout the ancient world, from Mesopotamia, Greece, the Middle East, and eventually into Europe, stone temples and monoliths were being erected to serve as religious institutions or places of worship. One example of an ancient temple is the Ziggurat, in what was ancient Mesopotamia. It is a rectangular, stepped tower, often surrounded by a temple. Ziggurats are believed to have first been erected in the third millennium BCE. Stepped pyramids have also been found in Central America, built by the ancient Mayans.

Information Organizations

Religious beliefs are commonly practiced on what is termed "sacred ground." For many religions, this is a church, temple, synagogue, etc. Some less organized religions practice their beliefs and rituals outdoors on ground that has special meaning or has been sanctified by a religious leader. Sanctifying means to purify the ground from any perceived evil.

Religions can also be perceived as religious organizations. The Catholic Church was founded in the first century, and later in the Byzantine Empire (330 -1453) after the Council of Nicene agreed on the canon for the Catholic religion, the church influenced kings and policy making, and still does to this day to some degree.

This is also the same for Islam, with its center in Mecca, and other religions around the world. Religion as an information organization not only provided ancient humans with a belief system that helped to explain many of the events happening around them, it also provided laws on societal behavior. To some extent, religion was necessary for prehistoric societies to evolve. Religious institutions also provided valuable information on current events that the population needed to know, like wars in far-off countries, or by passing messages along to other institutions affiliated with the same religion.

Religious Practices and Practitioners

Religious practices can include rituals, sermons, and commemoration/veneration of a deity or deities. In some cultures—Polynesian, Melanesian, and Maori, for example—a spiritual life-force energy permeates the universe and is the center of their belief system. This energy is called "mana." Religious practices do differ according to the beliefs of a particular faith. Some other practices can include sacrifices (Aztecs, to name one culture), feasts, festivals, trances, meditation, prayer, initiations, sacred dance, funerals, and matrimonial services. Some religious practices involve community service (Hare Krishna, for example).

What most religious practices have in common is that they are led by a recognized practitioner. How a leader in a religion is recognized can be by learning (seminary school or orally), being a chief or tribal leader, or being elected by a governing body or the society as a whole.

There are several types of religious practitioners, and followers often believe that these individuals are able to speak with the deity/deities directly. Others believe that their religious leaders have power given to them by "the gods." The ancient pharaohs of Egypt and their people believed that the pharaoh's power was given to him by the gods. Some types of religious practitioners include

- Shamans, who are individuals with access to supernatural power that can be used to benefit society or a single person. Shamans are most often found in indigenous cultures. The term "Shaman" originated with the Tungus people in eastern Siberia.
- Priests, who are trained religious practitioners that perform rituals for the benefit of the group. Unlike shamans, rituals are central for a priest. Creativity and in-

novation are strongly discouraged. Instead, priests are expected and required to follow set rules or creeds. Priests are in most organized religions; only their title changes. Some examples are rabbi, ministers, preachers, and monks.

- Sorcerers and witches, which do not have the same high regard in their societies as priests and shamans. This is usually because their abilities are seen to be negative or even "evil," according to some religious doctrine. Sorcerers (typically use tools) and witches (typically do not use tools) are believed by some to be able to connect to the supernatural. It is also believed that they can perform magic. Magic is the ability to do or control things, events, people, or nature without any scientifically proven methods. Wiccans are also considered to be a type of witch, although their main creed is to do no harm, only good. All three types of these religious practitioners are often well-versed in nature, mainly the properties of various plants. The term "witch" is over a thousand years old and comes from Old English. While belief in witches and shamans have existed since prehistory, throughout the ages these practitioners have frequently faced persecution. Two of the most infamous are the Spanish Inquisition and the Salem Witch Trials.

- Mediums are another type of religious practitioners that can connect with the spiritual. They often use possession and trances to heal or have divine answers to questions from the faithful.

Rituals

A ritual is defined as a sequence of gestures, words, actions, or objects that are performed in a predetermined place, typically one of worship, and a set order. Rituals are a feature of all known human cultures.

Rituals not only include worship rites and sacraments but also:

- rites of passage
- atonement
- oaths of allegiance
- purification rites
- coronations
- dedication ceremonies
- inaugurations (president)
- marriages, births, and funerals

Rituals are not only found in religion but in everyday cultural activities. Hand-shaking and other forms of greetings can also be viewed as rituals.

Religious rituals can be characterized by traditionalism, formalism, rule-governance, invariance, performance, and sacral symbolism, according to Catherine Bell, an American religious scholar.

Formalism

Anthropologists refer to the formalism in rituals as a "restricted code." This is the limited and rigidly organized sets of expressions used. Anthropologist Maurice Block states that a ritual urges participants to use a formal oratorical style of speech that is limited in syntax, vocabulary, intonation, and loudness, all of which are fixed in order. Since this type of speech limits what can be said, very little can be challenged by non-believers. Rituals also tend to support the traditional forms of social hierarchy.

Traditionalism

Rituals are traditional and their continuity helps to repeat historical precedent, mores, religious rites, and ceremonies accurately throughout generations. The difference between traditionalism and formalism is that the ritual may not be formal but it still follows the historical trend. One example is the American Thanksgiving holiday, where it might not be formal but still upholds the original tradition.

Invariance

A ritual is also invariant; it is a careful choreography. While this doesn't necessarily appeal to tradition, it does create timeless repetition. The center to invariance is body discipline. For example, during meditation or monastic prayer, it is meant to form moods and dispositions. Body discipline is often practiced in groups, e.g., monks in prayer or chanting.

Rule Governance

Rituals are normally governed by rules, similar to formalism. Rules are what impose the norms on behavior. In rituals, it either defines the limits of acceptable behavior or choreographs each move during the ritual.

Sacrifice

Sacrifice in rituals are activities that are performed that are appealing to divine or supernatural beings. Historically, it could've meant human sacrifice. The Aztec, Incan, and Mayan cultures of Mesoamerica, to name a few, would offer human and animal sacrifices to appease their gods. In modern history and times, it often means giving something up.

Sacrifice can also be a sacral symbol such as a flag, or in the Christian church, a sliver of wood from the cross Jesus was supposedly crucified on. Through a process of consecration or purifying, the object is deemed "holy" and separated from that which is not.

Performance

A ritual is a performance that creates a theater-like frame around the activities, events, and symbols that shape a person's experience. The ritual performance helps to simplify some of life's unanswerable questions by imposing a sense of order.

Applied Anthropology

Applied anthropology is defined as applying the theories and methods of anthropology to analyze and solve practical problems. Simply put, applied anthropology is the practical side of the field. It is research and data based and used to understand humans past and present.

The history of applied anthropology dates to the nineteenth century and British colonialism. During this time, the British government employed anthropologists to help with governing the colonies (by subjugating the local populations), and the anthropology methods and theories were being applied to benefit the employer and not the local people. This association with colonialism negatively affected applied anthropology until WWII, when the researchers were employed on both sides to help their respective war efforts. Some of the accomplishments of these applied anthropologists include:

- helping to establish governmental policy on food/supply rationing
- providing cultural data on both allies and adversaries

There are different views on what the role of an applied anthropologist should be, and this is still causing conflict in the scientific community. Some believe that anthropologists should focus on research, teaching, and publication—not practical matters. Others believe that applied anthropologists should only carry out policy, but not make or criticize it.

Still others feel that since anthropologists are considered "experts" on social change and human problems, that they should be permitted to make policies that affect individuals and/or society. This would require the anthropologist to:

1. identify what the populace perceives needs to be changed
2. work with the populace to create culturally and socially sensitive changes
3. protect the local populace from any change that is harmful or a "scheme"

An applied anthropologist also has several responsibilities that include ethical obligations to all peoples, species, and materials studied. The safety, dignity, and privacy of the species or humans must be protected and consent gained before the study begins.

Applied anthropologists also have a responsibility to science and the public. This includes conducting all studies with integrity, and preserving opportunities for future fieldworkers. Whenever possible, an applied anthropologist should discuss/publish/donate their work to the scholarly and scientific community. Their research should also be publicly available to anyone that wants to read it.

This modernization of applied anthropology, where scientific data became important, replaced the previously-held belief from colonialism after WWII and the subsequent "baby boom" that was the result of soldiers returning home and starting their own families. The children of the GIs not only helped fuel the economy, but also the American educational system. This was the start of the era of academic anthropology. By the 1970s, applied anthropologists were working with governments, businesses, hospitals, international organizations, and schools. Now, applied anthropology has niches in urban and medical studies. As societies continue to grow and evolve, applied anthropologists will most often be the ones that will be asked to apply their methods and theories to solve practical problems.

Some of the goals applied anthropologists use to develop successful programs today include:

- creating a program that is compatible with the indigenous culture
- using conceptual tools to identify cultural and social variations that are relevant to the creation and implementation of the program
- responding to the locally perceived need for change

- keeping programs simple, and avoiding over-innovation
- using traditional organizations and resources as much as possible (local labor, existing socio-political structures, etc.)
- ensuring the design to implement the program is flexible in order to fit society's needs while still being compatible with their culture

Cultural Preservation

Cultural preservation is the systematic efforts by anthropologists, historians, folklorists, and cultural geographers to protect the traditional customs, knowledge, materials, and natural resources of the culture. There are several primary goals associated with cultural preservation projects. These include:

- sustaining ecological and cultural diversity within communities and landscapes that are modernizing
- promoting active community involvement in managing local resources
- mobilizing government support to preserve regional (cultural) heritage

Traditional cultural resources can either be tangible or intangible. Some examples are

- tangible cultural resources like sacred landmarks, ethnic foods, vernacular architecture, and folk arts (painting, weaving, etc.)
- intangible cultural resources like storytelling, games, music, dance, and expressive oral traditions.

Cultural preservation also assesses the consequences of industrialization and relocation of cultural traditions that have symbolic and/or historical significance.

Recently, over the last few decades, cultural preservation has become more urgent as urban areas continue to grow. This is particularly true in the United States, where some people are giving up their traditional lifestyles in favor of a more "modern" one. When this occurs, anthropologists refer to it as "delocalization." One of the questions anthropologists now have to ask is what are the socioeconomic factors responsible for the loss of cultural heritage and traditions?

Several federally funded programs are active supporters of cultural preservation research. One of these programs is the National Endowment for the Humanities, and another is the American Folklife Center. Cultural preservation is most successful when a "grassroots" approach is taken. Cultural resources can be presented to the public as "living history." Some examples of this are:

- sea-grass baskets from coastal South Carolina
- Amish-made quilts from central Pennsylvania
- maple syrup from upstate Vermont
- woven blankets from the Navajo Nation

Even though promoting the sale of cultural resources may seem to undermine their authenticity, what is now known as "cultural tourism" can help ensure the rejuvenation of living traditions so they can continue to be passed down to future generations.

Directed Cultural Change

When one culture makes an effort to influence/change another culture, this is referred to as "directed cultural change." Over time, one culture spreads across another, eventually replacing that culture. In history, directed cultural change often occurred through military defeat or takeover. The conquering culture imposed their beliefs and traditions on the defeated one, often to help with submission. This was a common practice throughout ancient times, and even into colonialism.

An example of this would be when the Spanish conquered Central and South America, dispensing with the traditional cultural beliefs of the indigenous peoples (Aztecs, Mayans, and Incas). As another example, the British Empire directed cultural change throughout their colonies in India, Africa, Australia, etc.

Today, directed culture change can also refer to the culture at work. Various cultural identities are often employed and expected to perform their tasks together. This means that cultural traditions might have to be put aside, creating a new culture at work.

Spontaneous Cultural Change

A culture can change spontaneously due to social or environmental factors. This change is done normally to benefit society and can be influenced by outside sources (contact with another culture) or by a leader or group within their own.

A simple example of spontaneous culture change occurred with the introduction of the automobile. Not only was society able to move more freely around and over longer distances, it opened up the need for new labor skills, leaders, and education. Laborers were needed to build and maintain automobiles. Roads, bridges, and tunnels needed to be built for the new drivers. This also brought various cultures closer together, creating the opportunity for more changes in traditions.

Oil and gas also became extremely important commodities that are still influencing cultures around the world to this day. Middle Eastern cultures are interacting with Western ones, passing new ideas that are influencing additional change. For example, some Middle Eastern countries now allow women to drive and even vote, where previously it was strictly forbidden, even a decade ago.

Anthropologists that study cultural changes throughout the centuries have noted that it is not always bad. When new ideas and technology are introduced to a culture, it can have positive results, like women in some cultures being allowed more freedom.

Environment

Environmental anthropology examines humans and their relationship to the environment, and vice versa, in the past and present. In the 1960s, environmental anthropology had a breakthrough. There were several theories presented regarding functionalism and systems. The beginnings of the system theories were published in Seasonal Variations of the Eskimo by French sociologist Marcel Mauss. His system theories were later restated in part by Julian Steward.

While Marcel Mauss' system theories involved cultural materialism, social units are gauged by material production. Julian Steward acknowledged cultural patterns, or what he referred to as "laws." His ecological anthropology was based on climate, topography, resources, and how easily accessible they were to define the culture. Both presumed that culture was malleable and dependent on the environment. The social characteristics of the culture have limitations and are not considered determinants. These theories were later criticized for presuming societies were static.

This led to a new focus—environmental anthropology centered on cultural diversity and variation. Other factors were being observed that included:

- floods, earthquakes, frost, etc.
- migrations
- cost and benefit ratios
- contacts/associations
- trade and other external ideas
- internal, independent logic
- impact of inter-connectivity

There was still criticism over this approach to environmental anthropology, since it did not take into account such behaviors as loyalty and friendliness, along with any possible incentives or prohibitors that might influence behavior. Anthropologist Roy A. Rappaport, in response to criticism, remarked, "The social unit is not always well defined."

Today, according to the Society for Applied Anthropology (SAA), "Environmental anthropology is particularly effective in relating to and gaining understanding of cultural diversity in community settings, and intercultural/intersect oral conflict, thus lending itself to applied endeavors that involve collaboration among diverse interest groups for the common good."

Environmental anthropologists use a variety of tools and methods to address different problems. The SAA goes on to state that, "Important among them are observation techniques, qualitative and survey interviews, systematic data collection techniques for accessing core values or areas of cultural consensus, ways of identifying and interpreting social networks and a variety of participatory cultural, social and environmental assessment techniques designed to improve intersectoral understanding of demographic composition, social/political dynamics, cultural and other forms of diversity, and capacity for planning and development."

 Cultural Resource Management

Cultural resource management (CRM) is the career and practice of managing cultural resources like arts and heritage. It is concerned with traditional and historic culture, along with archaeology. CRM also focuses on current culture that includes innovative and progressive culture. Urban culture is one example.

Cultural resource management began in the 1960s and 1970s with the start of the environment/conservation movement. Legislation was passed during this time that focused on the protection of cultural resources. In 1974, the Archaeological and Historic Preservation Act (Moss-Bennett Act) was passed and helped start cultural management resources. It also created archaeological jobs in the federal government, private sector, and academia.

This wasn't the first act passed that dealt with managing cultural resources. In 1906, the Antiquities Act was passed. This act, signed by President Theodore Roosevelt, gave the president of the United States power to create national parks and monuments. However, it wasn't until the 1970s that the National Park Service started using the phrase "culture resources."

In 1974, two conferences were held: the Cultural Resource Management conference and Airlie House conference. After these conferences, the National Park Service defined CRM as:

"Those tangible and intangible aspects of cultural systems, both living and dead, that are valued by or representative of a given culture or that contain information about a culture…[They] include but are not limited to sites, structures, districts, objects, and historic documents associated with or representative of peoples, cultures, and human activities and events, either in the present or in the past. Cultural resources also can include primary written and verbal data for interpretation and understanding of those tangible resources."

In the 1970s, archaeologists began using CRM as a parallel to natural resource management and addressed the following resources:

- historic properties (listed/eligible for the National Register of Historic Places)
- older properties not registered but having cultural significance
- historic properties that also have cultural value
- archaeological graves and other cultural items
- shipwrecks
- historical documents
- museum collections
- religious sites and practices
- cultural use of natural resources
- folklife, tradition, and other social institutions
- orchestras, theater groups, and other cultural amenities

Much of the research and investigations conducted by archaeologists and anthropologists are on cultural sites that are threatened by development.

 Indigenous Survival and Global Culture

As early as the 1970s, anthropologists were advocating for the cultural survival of smaller populations that often lived in isolated areas that are rich in resources. This can make these cultures vulnerable to displacement and exploitation. An expanding indigenous rights movement in the 1980s provided a wide opening for anthropologists to become political advocates and cultural experts.

In the 1990s, anthropologists changed the term "cultural survival" to "globalization and local cultures." The question anthropologists were trying to answer now was how resilient are local cultures and are they able to "consume modernity" on their own terms?

This refers to if an indigenous people can maintain their culture, while also benefiting from modern technology.

Indian-American anthropologist Arjun Appadurai has put forth a comprehensive theory on globalization and what he has termed "public culture." Appadurai views culture as a "dimension of difference." He theorizes that global relations have more of a decisive bearing on human lives in today's world than their national identity. He goes on to note that this could be the start of the end of nation-states.

While a global or public culture has developed, anthropologists are not convinced that all cultures will blend into one. As of now, traditional societies still respond and assimilate modernity in their own ways, allowing anthropologists to research and document the culture and changes as they occur.

Sample Test Questions

1) What is anthropology?

   A) The study of evolution, human and animal.
   B) The study of past and present human cultures.
   C) The study of past and present humans, human behaviors, and societies.
   D) The study of ancient cultures.

The correct answer is C:) The study of past and present humans, human behaviors, and societies. Anthropology studies all aspects of human life through time.

2) Physical anthropology was changed to what name?

   A) Applied anthropology
   B) Biological anthropology
   C) Human biology
   D) Paleopathology

The correct answer is B:) Biological anthropology. Physical anthropology was changed to biological anthropology in response to Darwin's theory of evolution.

3) What is the 'Scala Naturae'?

   A) A scale that weighs natural materials.
   B) A hierarchy that lists the order of beings from deities to minerals.
   C) A list of natural plants.
   D) A natural scale.

The correct answer is B:) A hierarchy that lists the order of beings from deities to minerals. It is also referred to as the Great Chain of Being and was used by the ancient Greek philosopher Plato to create a hierarchy of beings, starting with deities, angels, humans, animals, plants, and finally minerals.

4) How many major human races did Johann Friedrich Blumenbach group his collection of skulls into?

   A) 5
   B) 3
   C) 7
   D) 4

The correct answer is A:) 5. Dr. Blumenbach divided the skulls into what he theorized were the five major human races: Caucasian, Mongolian, Aethiopian, Malayan, and American.

5) What does a monogenist believe?

   A) There were multiple ancestors for the five races.
   B) Some of the five races had the same ancestor.
   C) There was one common ancestor for the five known human races.
   D) Each of the five races had a different ancestor.

The correct answer is C:) There was one common ancestor for the five known human races. A monogenist believes that the five races represented by Dr. Blumenbach's skulls were derived from a single ancestor and then divided.

6) What does a polygenist believe?

   A) There is a single common ancestor for the five major races.
   B) Each race derived from a different ancestor.
   C) There were multiple ancestors for the five races.
   D) Some races had a common ancestor, while others did not.

The correct answer is B:) Each race derived from a different ancestor. A polygenist believes that each of the five proposed major races had a different ancestor.

7) Who is known as the "father of cultural anthropology"?

   A) Edward Sapir
   B) Lewis Henry Morgan
   C) Grafton Elliot Smith
   D) Franz Boas

The correct answer is D:) Franz Boas. German-American anthropologist Franz Boas is considered the "father of cultural anthropology." He believed that cultures were distinct and could not be compared to European standards.

8) Who was one of the founders of linguistic anthropology?

A) Edward Sapir
B) Dell Hymes
C) Ruth Benedict
D) William Cunnington

The correct answer is A:) Edward Sapir. Anthropologist Edward Sapir was one of the founders of linguistic anthropology and is known for his work researching the indigenous languages of the Americas.

9) What is ethnology?

A) The study of plants.
B) The study of an identifiable culture.
C) The study of fossils.
D) The study of the environment.

The correct answer is B:) The study of an identifiable culture. Ethnology, or cultural anthropology, is the study of an identifiable group of people. The writings by the researchers are called ethnographies.

10) What is holism?

A) The belief that a culture is greater as a whole than its individual parts
B) A great accomplishment by an individual is greater than the culture
C) A complete study on a culture
D) A study of a culture's religious beliefs

The correct answer is A:) The belief that a culture is greater as a whole than its individual parts. Holism is the idea that a culture as a whole is greater than an individual.

11) Fieldwork with Australian Aborigines depicted women as

A) Subservient in all aspects of life
B) Being dominant over men
C) Equal in all aspects of life
D) Active agents in all aspects of tribal life, except for politics

The correct answer is D:) Active agents in all aspects of tribal life, except for politics. Anthropologist Phyllis Kaberry's ethnographies showed that Aboriginal women had an active role in daily life, except for politics, which were decided by the culture's elders.

12) What is morphology?

   A) The study of a species' ability to change.
   B) The study of evolution.
   C) The study of a human to its structure.
   D) The study of morphine.

The correct answer is C:) The study of a human to its structure. Morphology is the study of a human to its structure and was the method commonly used to quantify human variation. An example of this would be Dr. Blumenbach's skulls.

13) What does the unilinear theory propose?

   A) All world cultures originated in Europe
   B) All cultures develop along the same path
   C) Cultures develop at different rates
   D) Cultures develop through gene and cultural evolution

The correct answer is B:) All cultures develop along the same path. The unilinear theory proposes that all cultures follow fixed stages of development that include savagery, barbarism, and civilization.

14) What are memetics?

   A) An idea that can jump from one mind to another, not the whole society.
   B) The study of images with catch-phrases.
   C) Copying ideas from one culture to another.
   D) An early form of rudimentary mathematics.

The correct answer is A:) An idea that can jump from one mind to another, not the whole society. Memetics are ideas that are spread without genes in a culture, usually vocally or through images. Memes tend to only "infect" a small number of individuals in a society. An example of this would be national terrorists.

15) What discovery is represented in Mendelian genetics?

   A) There are no patterns to genetics.
   B) Genes come in pairs.
   C) Genes are solo.
   D) Genes cannot be mapped.

The answer is B:) Genes come in pairs. Gregor Mendel, by studying pea plants, discovered that genes come in pairs.

16) What is cultural ecology?

   A) The theory that plants have their own cultures.
   B) The study of plants in a specific region.
   C) The theory that humans and their environment interact with each other equally.
   D) The theory that humans are separate from their environment.

The correct answer is C:) The theory that humans and their environment interact with each other equally. Cultural ecology theorizes that humans and their environment affect each other equally. Modern cultural ecologists still follow this theory, only now including political and others in the environment.

17) Early cultural evolutionists believed that these two aspects contributed to human evolution:

   A) Variation, natural selection
   B) Natural selection, environment
   C) Variation, environment
   D) Environment, genetics

The correct answer is A:) Variation, natural selection. Early cultural evolutionists closely followed Darwin's theory of evolution that proposed variation and natural selection contributed to human evolution and eventually language.

18) What is evolutionary epistemology?

   A) Human knowledge evolves at different stages.
   B) Parts of human knowledge develop according to selection.
   C) All humans develop the same knowledge.
   D) Knowledge develops according to the surrounding environment.

The correct answer is B:) Parts of human knowledge develop according to selection. Evolutionary epistemologists believe that parts of human knowledge, primarily scientific theories, evolve according to selection. Nature selects the best candidate, instead of knowledge being nurtured through experience.

19) What is the difference between "race" and "ethnicity"?

    A) Both terms have the same meaning.
    B) Race refers to physical characteristics and ethnicity refers to the cultural characteristics of the society.
    C) Ethnicity refers to skin color and race to a culture's geographical location.
    D) Race refers to physical characteristics and ethnicity to the surrounding environmental characteristics.

The correct answer is B:) Race refers to physical characteristics and ethnicity refers to the cultural characteristics of the society. Modern anthropologists lightly use the term race to describe physical characteristics, such as skin color. Ethnicity refers to the characteristics of the culture.

20) What was the eugenics movement of the 1920s?

    A) Promoted selective breeding to remove perceived "negative" traits
    B) An ancient form of exercise rediscovered in the early twentieth century
    C) Promoted breeding to increase populations
    D) Promoted limiting breeding to certain populations

The correct answer is A:) Promoted selective breeding to remove perceived "negative" traits. The eugenics movement promoted the idea of selective breeding to remove negative traits or increase the likelihood of positive ones. After the rise of Nazism, this movement rapidly fell out of favor.

21) What is primatology?

    A) An early name for anthropology
    B) The study of primates
    C) The study of the first humans
    D) The study of chimpanzees

The correct answer is B:) The study of primates. Primatology is the study of primates, extinct and living.

22) What are the two main types of primatology?

   A) Western and Japanese
   B) Western and European
   C) European and Japanese
   D) European and Asian

The correct answer is A:) Western and Japanese. There are two main types of primatology, Western and Japanese, though each has a different focus.

23) What is the primary function of a dominance hierarchy in a primate troop?

   A) One primate always has to feel "above" the others
   B) To help researchers track and identify their subjects
   C) To make it easier for the public to identify with a troop
   D) To maintain stability within the troop

The correct answer is D:) To maintain stability within the troop. The primary function of dominance hierarchy in a primate troop is to maintain its stability.

24) What is the definition of taxonomy?

   A) The art of stuffing and mounting deceased animals
   B) Another term for mummification
   C) A term for classifying organisms
   D) An ancient term for nation-state taxes

The correct answer is C:) A term for classifying organisms. Taxonomy is the classification of organisms and the "father of taxonomy" is considered to be Carl Linnaeus.

25) How much DNA do humans and chimpanzees share?

   A) 97–99%
   B) 50–60%
   C) 75%
   D) 80%

The correct answer is A:) 97–99%. Humans and chimpanzees share 97–99% DNA and are considered to be human's closest living "relative."

26) What is an epoch?

   A) A myth or story
   B) Part of an ethnography
   C) A specific period of time marked by notable events or certain characteristics
   D) A verb, similar to "epic"

The correct answer is C:) A specific period of time marked by notable events or certain characteristics. An epoch is a specific period of time marked by notable events or certain characteristics. An example of this would be the period during the last ice age.

27) What is paleontology?

   A) The study of dinosaurs
   B) The study of life before and during the Holocene Epoch
   C) The study of fossils
   D) The study of light colored species

The correct answer is B:) The study of life before and during the Holocene Epoch. Paleontologists study life that existed before and sometimes during the Holocene Epoch. This is the epoch that began after the last glacial period, approximately 11,700 years before the present date.

28) How many elements are there to paleontology research?

   A) 5
   B) 3
   C) 7
   D) 2

The correct answer is B:) 3. There are three elements to paleontology research that include describing past events, developing an explainable theory, and applying the theory to facts.

29) What are the three types of fossils?

   A) Wood, bone, shells
   B) Bone, wood, rock
   C) Bone, rock, minerals
   D) Bone, rock, shells

The correct answer is A:) Wood, bone, shells. Paleontologists study wood, bone, and shell fossils, typically using radiocarbon dating to approximate their age.

30) What is radiocarbon dating?

   A) A method for dating the age of an object by measuring the rates radioactive elements decay
   B) How anthropologists date a culture's age
   C) A method used to date specific types of technology
   D) Methods used by ancient cultures to track dates

The correct answer is A:) A method for dating the age of an object by measuring the rates radioactive elements decay. Paleontologists use radiocarbon dating to determine the age of fossils and other artifacts. If radioactive elements aren't present, stratigraphy can also be used. This is using the layers of sediment where the object was found to form an approximate date.

31) What is a Cnidarian?

   A) An early human culture
   B) The name of an ancient city
   C) The earliest known animal
   D) An ancient religious text

The correct answer is C:) The earliest known animal. Cnidarians lived approximately 580 million years ago in fresh and marine environments and are believed to be the first known animal.

32) What are archosaurs?

   A) Prehistoric vertebrates
   B) A species of dinosaur, similar to the "T-Rex"
   C) Prehistoric vegetation
   D) An early species of jellyfish

The correct answer is A:) Prehistoric vertebrates. Archosaurs did include the dinosaurs, along with other vertebrates. It does not refer to a specific species of dinosaur.

33) What is stratigraphic excavation?

   A) Drawing a graph of an excavation site
   B) An excavation that has published graphs associated with it
   C) Using specialized tools for an excavation
   D) The careful removal of each layer of dirt

The correct answer is D:) The careful removal of each layer of dirt. In a stratigraphic excavation, each layer of dirt at the site is carefully removed to preserve the site's features. One of the first examples of a stratigraphic excavation can be seen at Pompeii.

34) Who is known as the "father of the big dig"?

   A) Giuseppe Fiorelli
   B) Heinrich Schliemann
   C) Ernst Curtius
   D) William Matthew Flinders Petrie

The correct answer is C:) Ernst Curtius. Anthropologist Ernst Curtius became known as the "father of the big dig" during and after his excavations at Greece's Olympus.

35) Where were humans primarily located during the Paleolithic era?

   A) Asia
   B) Middle East
   C) Mesoamerica
   D) Eastern Africa

The correct answer is D:) Eastern Africa. During the Paleolithic period, humans were primarily centered in eastern Africa, with an estimated one person per square mile.

36) Why did human populations start settling down?

   A) Agriculture
   B) Sudden population explosion
   C) New technology/inventions were created
   D) Climate change

The correct answer is A:) Agriculture. Once small hunter-gatherer bands began cultivating seeds on a small scale, society changed and started to become more sedentary.

37) What were the first humans to walk upright?

   A) Homo sapiens
   B) Homo erectus
   C) Homo neanderthalensis
   D) Homo heidelbergensis

The correct answer is B:) Homo erectus. Homo erectus are believed to be the first humans to walk upright.

38) When was the Java Man discovered?

   A) 1891
   B) 1922
   C) 1871
   D) 1962

The correct answer is A:) 1891. The Java Man was discovered in 1891 and dates to approximately 700,000–100,000,000 BCE.

39) When was Peking Man discovered?

   A) 1947
   B) 1937
   C) 1891
   D) 1967

The correct answer is B:) 1937. Peking Man was discovered near Beijing, China between 1929 and 1937.

40) What is the age of the oldest human fossil discovered in the United States?

   A) 100,000 years
   B) 60,000 years
   C) 16,500 years
   D) 30,000 years

The correct answer is C:) 16,500. Currently, the oldest known human fossil discovered in the U.S. dates back 16,500 years.

41) Australopithecus was the first to do what?

    A) Grow crops
    B) Domesticate animals
    C) Erect megaliths
    D) Use stone tools

The correct answer is D:) Use stone tools. These early human ancestors are believed to be the first to use crude stone tools.

42) What are Clovis and Folsom points?

    A) Ancient navigation points in the sky
    B) A type of gesture used by ancient cultures
    C) Types of tools used in hunting
    D) An agricultural tool

The correct answer is C:) Types of tools used in hunting. Clovis and Folsom points were used by hunters, similar to spear points, to bring down large game.

43) What are the five components needed for a society to be a culture?

    A) Language, land, artifacts, beliefs, architecture
    B) Language, symbols, beliefs, norms, and artifacts
    C) Artifacts, architecture, language, customs, norms
    D) Architecture, language, norms, customs, land

The correct answer is B:) Language, symbols, beliefs, norms, and artifacts. For a society to be considered a culture, it must have language, symbols, beliefs, norms, and artifacts.

44) What are norms?

    A) Normal behavior
    B) Type of cultural food
    C) Laws
    D) Social class

The correct answer is C:) Laws. Norms are the laws that regulate society's behavior.

45) What was Edward Sapir's contribution to anthropology?

   A) Helped develop the discipline of anthropologic linguistics
   B) Discovered the location of Troy
   C) Excavated Olympus
   D) Extensively studied primates

The correct answer is A:) Helped develop the discipline of anthropologic linguistics. Edward Sapir helped develop the methods used by linguists.

46) What is the name for the first human language?

   A) First language
   B) Primary language
   C) Proto-Human
   D) Proto-Language

The correct answer is C:) Proto-Human. The first form of human language (Proto-Human) was thought to have developed around 50,000 to 150,000 years ago.

47) What is the earliest form of writing

   A) Pre-cuneiform
   B) Hieroglyphics
   C) Pictographs
   D) Cuneiform

The correct answer is A:) Pre-cuneiform. First used by the Sumerians it is similar in form to hieroglyphics used by the ancient Egyptians.

48) What is the study of time in nonverbal communication called?

   A) Proxemics
   B) Chronology
   C) Kinesics
   D) Chronemics

The correct answer is D:) Chronemics is the study of time and how its used during nonverbal communication.

49) What is a symbolic system?

   A) A system in name only
   B) A collection of symbols
   C) A system used to categorize symbols
   D) An ancient system of government

The correct answer is A:) A system in name only. A symbolic system is not tangible but is passed down through generations. Currency is an example of a symbolic system.

50) What is proxemics?

   A) Study of microorganisms
   B) Amount of space needed for comfort
   C) The study of conversational pauses
   D) A form of energy

The correct answer is B:) Amount of space needed for comfort. Proxemics refers to the amount of personal space an individual needs to feel comfortable.

51) How many types of sign language are there?

   A) 7
   B) 3
   C) 5
   D) 1

The correct answer is C:) 5. There are five types of sign languages: American, French, Ethiopian, Spanish, and Arabic.

52) What is cultural diffusion?

   A) The dismantling of a culture
   B) When a culture gets rid of its belief system
   C) Settling a disagreement between two cultures
   D) The spread of ideas from one culture to another

The correct answer is D:) The spread of ideas from one culture to another. Cultural diffusion occurs when ideas are spread from one culture to another.

53) What does "taboo" refer to?

   A) An act/item that is socially and culturally abhorrent
   B) A type of ritual tattoo
   C) A cultural food
   D) A style of dance

The correct answer is A:) An act/item that is socially and culturally abhorrent. Taboo is an act or item that is morally offensive to the culture.

54) What is colonialism?

   A) A style of home
   B) To extend power over a weaker culture
   C) A style of art
   D) When two cultures join together

The correct answer is B:) To extend power over a weaker culture. Colonialism is when one culture extends power over a weaker one, often for resources.

55) When were megalithic architecture first erected?

   A) Bronze Age
   B) Neolithic Period
   C) Paleolithic Period
   D) Iron Age

The correct answer is B:) Neolithic Period. Megaliths have been dated to approximately 8000 BCE and possibly further back in history.

56) What are cross-cousins?

   A) Two cousins each from a brother and sister
   B) Two cousins from the father's side
   C) Two cousins from the mother's side
   D) Not related by blood

The correct answer is A:) Two cousins each from a brother and sister. Cross-cousins are from a brother and sister. In cultures where cousins commonly marry, this is often the preferred blood relationship due to a slightly weaker family tie.

57) What are the types of political organizations?

   A) Bands, hunter-gatherers, tribes, chiefdoms
   B) Bands, agriculture, states, tribes
   C) Bands, tribes, chiefdoms, states
   D) Bands, villages, cities, nations

The correct answer is C:) Bands, tribes, chiefdoms, states. Known as sociopolitical typology, the four types of organizations are bands, tribes, chiefdoms, and states, also known as hunter-gatherers, horticulture, pastoralism, and agriculture respectively.

58) What is horticulture?

   A) A culture that worships plants
   B) The study of a culture's environment
   C) Large-scale farming
   D) Growing plants for multiple uses

The correct answer is D:) Growing plants for multiple uses. Horticulture is the second level of a political organization, when a culture grows plants for food, materials, decoration, etc. It is believed the start of horticulture changed hunter-gatherer bands into tribes.

59) What were the first domesticated animals?

   A) Horses
   B) Pigs
   C) Dogs
   D) Cows

The correct answer is B:) Pigs. The first animals domesticated are believed to be pigs, in Mesopotamia around 11,000 BCE.

60) There are how many types of states?

   A) 3
   B) 5
   C) 1
   D) 9

The correct answer is A:) 3. There are three types of states: sovereign, hegemony, and federal.

61) What was the first Mesoamerican civilization?

A) Inca
B) Aztec
C) Olmec
D) Mayan

The correct answer is D:) Mayan. Anthropologists believe that the Mayans were the first Mesoamerican civilization, beginning around 2600 BCE.

62) Which civilization invented "zero"?

A) Sumerians
B) Olmec
C) Persians
D) Egyptians

The correct answer is A:) Sumerians. The Sumerians are believed to be the first culture to use "zero," though it was later "rediscovered" in India around 628 BCE.

63) What was the youngest city-state in Mesoamerica?

A) Inca
B) Aztecs
C) Mayan
D) Olmec

The correct answer is B:) Aztecs. The Aztecs were the youngest city-state in Mesoamerican before the Spanish invasion in 1533.

64) Who built Chichen Itza?

A) Inca
B) Aztec
C) Mayans
D) Olmec

The correct answer is C:) Mayans. Chichen Itza was the largest city built by the Mayans and was occupied from around 600 to 1221 AD.

65) Who built Tenochtitlan?

    A) Aztecs
    B) Olmecs
    C) Inca
    D) Mayan

The correct answer is A:) Aztecs. The Aztecs built Tenochtitlan around 1325 AD.

66) What was the Inca culture missing?

    A) Cities
    B) Resources
    C) Artifacts
    D) Writing

The correct answer is D:) Writing. The Inca used symbols and oral traditions instead of writing.

67) What is the oldest subsistence program?

    A) Horticulture
    B) Foraging
    C) Hunting
    D) Herding

The correct answer is B:) Foraging. The oldest subsistence program was foraging and it was relied on by ancient human societies up to 10,000 years ago.

68) What is reciprocity?

    A) Gift-giving
    B) Bartering
    C) Trade
    D) Commerce

The correct answer is A:) Gift-giving. Reciprocity is the act of giving a gift and receiving one in return.

69) There are how many types of reciprocity?

   A) 2
   B) 3
   C) 4
   D) 1

The correct answer is B:) 3. There are three types of reciprocity: generalized, balanced, and negative.

70) What was the first crop cultivated?

   A) Rice
   B) Peas
   C) Rye
   D) Wheat

The correct answer is D:) Wheat. One of the first crops grown was wheat and can be dated back to at least 10,000 years ago.

71) Religious beliefs can be classified into which three categories?

   A) Fundamentalism, orthodoxy, reform
   B) Fundamentalism, reform, new-age
   C) Reform, orthodoxy, liberal
   D) Orthodoxy, liberal, fundamentalism

The correct answer is A:) Fundamentalism, orthodoxy, reform. Religious beliefs are classified as fundamentalism, orthodoxy, and reform.

72) When was the term "fundamentalist" first used?

   A) In the Middle Ages
   B) During the Protestant Reformation
   C) In the twentieth century
   D) During the 1800s

The correct answer is C:) In the twentieth century. The term "fundamentalist" was first used in the twentieth century to describe anti-modern Protestants in the United States.

73) What is a myth?

- A) A traditional story of events that explains a practice, belief, or natural phenomenon
- B) A person or thing with an unverified existence or that is imaginary
- C) A metaphor for the spiritual potentiality in humans
- D) All of the above

The correct answer is D:) All of the above. There are three possible definitions for mythology, though the most well-known is as a traditional story.

74) What event helped to create organized religion?

- A) Agriculture
- B) Natural disaster
- C) Development of language
- D) Evolution

The correct answer is A:) Agriculture. With large-scale agriculture, city-states developed. A larger population allowed for religion to become cohesive and more complex.

75) What is the oldest known organized religion still in practice?

- A) Christianity
- B) Judaism
- C) Islam
- D) Hinduism

The correct answer is D:) Hinduism. The religion known as Hinduism can be traced back 4,000 to 5,000 years ago.

76) What is a cargo cult?

- A) A group of people that worship cargo
- B) A religion that calls on the gods to deliver modern goods
- C) A culture that worships ships
- D) A group of people that work in shipping

The correct answer is B:) A religion that calls on the gods to deliver modern goods. Cargo cults are typically found in under-developed cultures that ask the spirits to send technologically advanced goods.

77) When did the first known human burial occur?

   A) 100,000 BCE
   B) 150,000 BCE
   C) 10,000 BCE
   D) 15,000 BCE

The correct answer is A:) 100,000 BCE. The earliest known human burial dates to 100,000 BCE in the Middle East.

78) What is a ziggurat?

   A) A weapon
   B) Mythical animal
   C) Stepped pyramid
   D) Type of food

The correct answer is C:) Stepped pyramid. A ziggurat is a stepped pyramid used as a temple or bureaucratic office. Two examples of ziggurats can be found in Central America and in modern day Iraq.

79) Where did the term "shaman" originate?

   A) Mesoamerica
   B) Mesopotamia
   C) Australia
   D) Siberia

The correct answer is D:) Siberia. The term "shaman" originated in Siberia with the Tungus people.

80) Where did the term "witch" originate?

   A) America
   B) Egypt
   C) Africa
   D) Europe (England)

The correct answer is D:) Europe (England). The term "witch" is derived from Old English and dates back about a thousand years.

81) What is sacrifice in religion?

   A) A feast
   B) A religious offering
   C) A blessing
   D) A creed

The correct answer is B:) A religious offering. A sacrifice is offering something that has been given up. Some cultures required individuals and animals to give up their lives to appease the gods or to win favor with the deities.

82) What is an attempt to control supernatural forces through the performance of a ritual that ensures clearly defined outcomes?

   A) Debate
   B) Election
   C) Religion
   D) Séance

The correct answer is C:) Religion. Almost all recognized religions seek to control supernatural forces through rituals that are designed to produce a clearly defined outcome.

83) What is mana?

   A) Spiritual energy
   B) Wafer cakes
   C) Water
   D) Spiritual life-force energy

The correct answer is D:) Spiritual life-force energy. Mana is the spiritual life-force energy that some cultures believe surrounds everything in the universe.

84) Trained religious leaders are often called

   A) Priests
   B) Witches
   C) Shamans
   D) Mediums

The correct answer is A:) Priests. Trained religious officials are often called priests. However, rabbis, ministers, preachers, and monks are also trained religious leaders.

85) When did applied anthropology become a science?

A) 1700s
B) 1800s
C) 1900s
D) 1600s

The correct answer is B:) 1800s. Applied anthropology dates to British colonialism in the nineteenth century.

86) What is an example of a tangible cultural resource?

A) Music
B) Symbols
C) Facial expressions
D) Sacred landmarks

The correct answer is D:) Sacred landmarks. One example of a tangible cultural resource is sacred landmarks.

87) What is an example of an intangible cultural resource?

A) Stories
B) Money
C) Food
D) Arts

The correct answer is A:) Stories. Stories and story-telling are one example of an intangible cultural resource.

88) What is "cultural tourism"?

A) Sightseeing
B) Selling cultural resources
C) Taking a trip
D) Visiting different cultures

The correct answer is B:) Selling cultural resources. To protect cultures, some sell specific items that are relevant to their culture. One example would be blankets woven by the Navajo Nation.

89) What is directed cultural change?

   A) A culture chooses to change voluntarily
   B) The surrounding environment forces a change
   C) One culture is influenced by another
   D) The society's leader decides to change the culture

The correct answer is C:) One culture is influenced by another. Directed cultural change occurs when one culture is influenced or dominated by another.

90) What is spontaneous cultural change?

   A) Change is forced by social or environmental factors
   B) Change occurs due to another culture's influence
   C) The society's leader suddenly decides to change the culture
   D) Society decides to change as a whole

The correct answer is A:) Change is forced by social or environmental factors. Spontaneous cultural change is typically forced by environmental or social changes that happen suddenly.

91) Environmental anthropology examines

   A) Environmental changes
   B) How humans and their environment react to each other
   C) The history of earth's environment
   D) How the environment affects history

The correct answer is B:) How humans and their environment react to each other. Environmental anthropology studies how humans and the environment interact and react to each other.

92) CRM is the acronym for what in anthropology?

   A) Customer relationship management
   B) Canadian resource management
   C) Cost of resource management
   D) Cultural resource management

The correct answer is D:) Cultural resource management. CRM is the acronym for cultural resource management.

93) In what year was the Archaeological and Historic Preservation Act Passed?

   A) 1889
   B) 1974
   C) 1984
   D) 1997

The correct answer is B:) 1974. The act was passed in 1974 and was the start of cultural resource management.

94) What is cultural resource management?

   A) The protection of a culture's resources
   B) Managing natural resources
   C) An administrative office that regulates water and power
   D) An official title

The correct answer is A:) The protection of a culture's resources. The purpose of cultural resource management is to protect vulnerable cultures' history, traditions, languages, beliefs, etc.

95) What is public culture?

   A) The culture of a public official
   B) The globalization of culture
   C) A highly visible culture
   D) Traditions/rituals that are only performed in public

The correct answer is B:) The globalization of culture. Public culture refers to the globalization of cultures as the world becomes more connected.

96) In cultural materialism, social units are gauged by what?

   A) Their possessions
   B) What they require
   C) Materials produced
   D) Cost of materials

The correct answer is C:) Materials produced. In the theory of cultural materialism, social units in a society are gauged by material production.

97) The acronym SAA stands for what?

A) Society for Applied Anthropology
B) Social Anthropology and Archaeology
C) Society for Anthropological Advancements
D) Society for Applied Archaeology

The correct answer is A:) Society for Applied Anthropology. SAA is the acronym for the Society for Applied Anthropology.

98) The end of what world event helped start the era of academic anthropology?

A) WWI
B) The discovery by the Western world of the Great Pyramids
C) WWII
D) The discovery of the first human fossil

The correct answer is C:) WWII. The end of WWII and the subsequent baby boom helped start a new era for anthropology.

99) An example of a modern culture today is what?

A) Culture at work
B) Culture in religion
C) Political culture
D) Folklore

The answer is A:) Culture at work. One example of a modern culture is the one that is developed at the workplace.

100) What did the term "cultural survival" change to?

A) Globalization and local cultures
B) Global cultures
C) Preserve global cultures
D) Local cultures and the world

The correct answer is A:) Globalization and local cultures. In the 1990s, the term was changed to "globalization and local cultures" to describe the threat that world intrusion has on a society, often one that is isolated.

Test Taking Strategies

Here are some test-taking strategies that are specific to this test and to other DSST tests in general:

- Keep your eyes on the time. Pay attention to how much time you have left.

- Read the entire question and read all the answers. Many questions are not as hard to answer as they may seem. Sometimes, a difficult sounding question really only is asking you how to read an accompanying chart. Chart and graph questions are on most DANTES/DSST tests and should be an easy free point.

- If you don't know the answer immediately, the new computer-based testing lets you mark questions and come back to them later if you have time.

- Read the wording carefully. Some words can give you hints to the right answer. There are no exceptions to an answer when there are words in the question such as always, all or none. If one of the answer choices includes most or some of the right answers, but not all, then that is not the answer. Here is an example:

    The primary colors include all of the following:
    A)   Red, Yellow, Blue, Green
    B)   Red, Green, Yellow
    C)   Red, Orange, Yellow
    D)   Red, Yellow, Blue

    Although item A includes all the right answers, it also includes an incorrect answer, making it incorrect. If you didn't read it carefully, were in a hurry, or didn't know the material well, you might fall for this.

- Make a guess on a question that you do not know the answer to. There is no penalty for an incorrect answer. Eliminate the answer choices that you know are incorrect. For example, this will let your guess be a 1 in 3 chance instead.

 ## *What Your Score Means*

Based on your score, you may, or may not, qualify for credit at your specific institution. The current ACE recommended score for this exam is 46. Your school may require a higher or lower score to receive credit. To find out what score you need for credit, you need to get that information from your school's website or academic advisor.

You lose no points for incorrect questions so make sure you answer each question. If you don't know, make an educated guess. On this particular test, you must answer 100 questions in 90 minutes.

Test Preparation

How much you need to study depends on your knowledge of a subject area. If you are interested in literature, took it in school, or enjoy reading then your study and preparation for the literature or humanities test will not need to be as intensive as that of someone who is new to literature.

This book is much different than the regular DSST study guides. This book actually teaches you the information that you need to know to pass the test. If you are particularly interested in an area, or feel that you want more information, do a quick search online. We've tried not to include too much depth in areas that are not as essential on the test. It is important to understand all major theories and concepts listed in the table of contents. It is also important to know any bolded words.

Don't worry if you do not understand or know a lot about the area. With minimal study, you can complete and pass the test.

We use test questions to teach you new information not covered in the study guide AND to test your knowledge of items you should already know from reading the text. If you don't know the answer to the test question, review the material. If it is new information, then this is an area that will be covered on the test but not in detail.

To prepare for the test, make a series of goals. Set aside a certain amount of time to review the information you have already studied and to learn additional material. Take notes as you study; it will help you learn the material. If you haven't done so already, download the study tips guide from the website and use it to start your study plan.

Legal Note

All rights reserved. This Study Guide, Book and Flashcards are protected under US Copyright Law. No part of this book or study guide or flashcards may be reproduced, distributed or stored in a retrieval system, or transmitted in any form or by any means, electronic, mechanical, photocopying, recording, or otherwise, without the prior written permission of the publisher Breely Crush Publishing LLC.

DSST is a registered trademark of Prometric and its affiliated companies, and does not endorse this book.

FLASHCARDS

This section contains flashcards for you to use to further your understanding of the material and test yourself on important concepts, names or dates. Read the term or question then flip the page over to check the answer on the back. Keep in mind that this information may not be covered in the text of the study guide. Take your time to study the flashcards, you will need to know and understand these concepts to pass the test.

Anthropology	How many types of sign language?
Australopithecus	What year was the Archaeological and Historic Preservation Act Passed?
Oldest human fossil discovered in the United States	Edward Sapir
Radiocarbon dating	Epoch

5	The study of past and present humans, human behaviors, and societies
1974	First to use stone tools
A founder of linguistic anthropology	16,500 years
A specific period of time marked by notable events or certain characteristics	A method for dating the age of an object by measuring the rates radioactive elements decay

Taboo

Unilinear theory

Proxemics

Memetics

Edward Sapir

Taxonomy

CRM

Father of the big dig

All cultures develop along the same path	Act/item that is socially and culturally abhorrent
An idea that can jump from one mind to another, not the whole society	Amount of space needed for comfort
Classifying organisms	Anthropologic linguistics
Ernst Curtius	Cultural resource management

Franz Boas	**Homo erectus**
Proto-Human	**When was the Java Man discovered?**
Cultural survival	**Scala Naturae**
Norms	**Hinduism**

First humans to walk upright	Father of cultural anthropology
1891	First language
Great Chain of Being	Globalization and local cultures
Oldest known organized religion still in practice	Laws that regulate society's behavior

Evolutionary epistemology	Archosaurs
Sacrifice	Tangible cultural resource
Cultural tourism	The term shaman came from what country?
SAA	Mana

Prehistoric vertebrates	Parts of human knowledge develop according to selection
Sacred landmarks	Religious offering
Siberia	Selling cultural resources
Spiritual life-force energy	Society for Applied Anthropology

Ziggurat	**Symbolic system**
Holism	**Stratigraphic excavation**
Cnidarian	**Cultural diffusion**
Morphology	**Ethnology**

System in name only	Stepped pyramid
The careful removal of each layer of dirt	The belief that a culture is greater as a whole than its individual parts
The spread of ideas from one culture to another	The earliest known animal
The study of an identifiable culture	The study of a human to its structure

Paleontology	Primatology
Cultural ecology	Monogenist
Priests	Clovis and Folsom points
Two main types of primatology	Three types of fossils

The study of primates	The study of life before and during the Holocene Epoch
There was one common ancestor for the five known human races	The theory that humans and their environment interact with each other equally
Types of tools used in hunting	Trained religious officials
Wood, bone, shells	Western and Japanese

NOTES

NOTES

NOTES

NOTES

NOTES

NOTES

www.ingramcontent.com/pod-product-compliance
Lightning Source LLC
Chambersburg PA
CBHW081832300426

44116CB00014B/2567